MW01274868

Legacy
Letters

Backstory Synopsis

After thirty-five years of journaling her true accounts of love and marriage, and the joys of family life experiences, Stephanie Livingston came to a crisis that brought her life to a crossroads, where she questioned everything.

Who am I and who do I want to be when I come through to the other side of this great chasm of loss and pain that is before me?

What's my purpose and my new identity now? Where did this all begin? When will this hurt and pain end? How do I sort through the mess this turbulent storm left behind in the hope of finding something beautiful once again, and why did God allow me to go through this trial?

At times, we're all faced with the uncomfortable new place of being alone and the fears that come from life's losses and changes. It's in questioning everything, reflecting on her past, and speaking to her younger self that the author finds healing and discovers deeper truths and purpose. The Holy Spirit speaks to her in her dreams, and she embraces God's will, His voice, and His Word to lead her, reshape her, and prepare her for a new thing He is about to do in her life.

Legacy Letters

True Memoirs of
Love, Marriage, Family,
and the Hopeful Journey
through Betrayal
and Loss

STEPHANIE LIVINGSTON

WESTBOW
P R E S S®
A DIVISION OF THOMAS NELSON
& ZONDERVAN

WestBow Press books may be ordered through booksellers or by contacting:

WestBow Press
A Division of Thomas Nelson & Zondervan
1663 Liberty Drive
Bloomington, IN 47403
www.westbowpress.com
844-714-3454

ISBN: 979-8-3850-2204-5 (sc)
ISBN: 979-8-3850-2205-2 (hc)
ISBN: 979-8-3850-2206-9 (e)

Library of Congress Control Number: 2024906245

Print information available on the last page.

WestBow Press rev. date: 10/16/2024

To My Darling Children and Grandchildren,

My heart is full of love and inspiration because God gifted you to me. I dedicate my story, our story to you and hope that one day you too will pen your words and sing your songs to leave your echo for generations to come. Don't be shy, express your little hearts out in love, music, and dance, for we have nothing but this moment we call 'now' in time. Use your voice and live out loud. May the lines that shape your eyes and the callouses on your hands be a testament and remembrance of the indescribable joy, laughter, labor, and tears we shared here on earth.

Don't forget to wish upon that star and pray to your heavenly Father. Live your dreams, pursue your good passions, and always remember your favorite things, like raindrops on roses and whiskers on kittens.

CONTENTS

Introduction   xi

Chapter 1   Coffee with God   1
Chapter 2   The Prince and the Promise   5
Chapter 3   The New Identity and the Lost-Teeth Dream: 1987   10
Chapter 4   The Light that Shines in the Dark: June 2022   16
Chapter 5   Finishing Well: 2022   21
Chapter 6   A Letter from a Mother's Heart   24
Chapter 7   The Shabby and the Chic   30
Chapter 8   Double Joy   36
Chapter 9   A Beautiful Mess   40
Chapter 10   For the Love of Family   47
Chapter 11   The Third Thrill   50
Chapter 12   The Degrees of Love, Pursuits, and
             Family: March 1995   58
Chapter 13   When the Cat's Away, the Mice Will Play   67
Chapter 14   The View from My Rocking Chair   84
Chapter 15   A Few Really Bad and Good-for-Nothing Days   91
Chapter 16   Fall from Grace   98
Chapter 17   New Beginnings: January 1, 1998   111
Chapter 18   The Jungle Dream: February 1999   124
Chapter 19   Happy Saturday: January 2002   135
Chapter 20   Back to School in a New Country   138
Chapter 21   A Warning Call for Purity   146

Chapter 22 The Stronghold: September 2008   150

Chapter 23 Keep on Keep'n On: 2006/2008   159

Chapter 24 The Way Back Home: 2012   166

Chapter 25 Blessed or Cursed in the Valley of Floods: 20018/2019   171

Chapter 26 Absence of Full Disclosure: Spring of 2020   181

Chapter 27 Bewitched Descent: February 2023   185

Chapter 28 The Dark Alley of Fear: Spring 2020   193

Chapter 29 Still Romance in Rest and Work: Summer 2020   197

Chapter 30 Deception Intersection: Fall 2021   201

Chapter 31 Who Stole the Cookies from the Cookie Jar?   224

Chapter 32 The Entangled Heart and Mind: February 2023   230

Chapter 33 The Grateful Pause   235

Chapter 34 This New Stop in Quiet and Hope: Spring, 2022   238

Chapter 35 Decking His Halls with Her Boughs of Holly: December 2022   252

Chapter 36 Family Christmas at the Farm: December 2022–January 2023   260

Chapter 37 The Courtroom of Justice: Winter 2023   276

Chapter 38 The Complication of This Grief   283

Chapter 39 There's No Crime in Crimson: April 2023   291

Chapter 40 The Reflection in the Mirror   297

Chapter 41 The Severed Heart: February 2023   312

Chapter 42 Legacy of Wisdom, Courage, Grace, Honor, and Worth: February 2023   322

Chapter 43 Red Flags of Hurt, Hunger, Hiding, and Healing with the White Flag of Surrender   352

Chapter 44 A Glimpse of Heaven   375

Chapter 45 The Awakening: September 5, 2023   393

INTRODUCTION

I am a wife, a mom, a daughter, a sister, and a friend, but most of all, I've come to realize that my life, in all its love and pain, has purpose and won't go without cause. Because, in this knowing, I take pause and stop through it all to read the Good Book, to pen out an inkling in time, to somehow make sense of the memories we leave for the future generations to come. May those who've gone behind us find us faithful and the past we leave behind shape us into people of promise and individuals who choose to live a life of love and honorable legacy.

One day, through time, I could possibly sit down with a coffee or tea in hand to speak to the younger me and to hopefully be the grandma who gleaned the best from my experiences as an individual who sorted out the broken pieces of life and turned the tragedies and this mess into a beautiful mosaic of memories and pictures of us.

I journal and write the letters and words that echo our time that will soon pass by, ever so quickly. We all have experienced days of joy, hardship, regret, laughter, and tears. So what will we make of this beautiful mess?

My only hope and prayer is, this mess of memories will be our message, and life's tests will turn into our testimony. Hopefully, when we go through life's refining fires and know this one truth for sure, the truth that we have a good God Who loves us and will help us through. God is love. He will always stay, and He will never leave us or forsake us. Through Jesus Christ, our Savior, we can experience a redeeming love that reaches beyond our failures so He can still grow something fruitful with our burnt ashes.

I write, not in the shame of exposure or regret, but in the light that shines truth in dark places. I write these journals of secret honesty to share my journey and to become a voice that speaks honor and truth with our children, and their children, and anyone who cares to read and understand this beautiful thing we call marriage, family, and life. I write so you can learn from our mistakes, and I hope you choose a better path by not giving up on this valuable thing called love and marriage.

> Know also that wisdom is like honey for
> you: If you find it, there is a future hope
> for you, and your hope will not be cut off.
> —Proverbs 24:14

Chapter 1

COFFEE WITH GOD

May 2022

Who am I now? I wonder as I sit alone this morning while I open the black-and-white leopard-print box containing letters and words held within the pages of twelve journals that explore decades of marriage and memories. Do my private diaries and penned entries about the younger me, my husband, my children, and prayers to my God give any understanding as to why we're even here? Could my recounted words and dreams give any understanding to anyone who reads or may divinely encounter my life filled with joy, laughter, dreams, pain, and betrayal? Could you relate to my journey, and would you care to open your heart to the depths that may still envelop the mysteries of the secret self?

I look out from the deck of my small condo and sip my coffee on this chilly and blustery spring day. The unusually cool, cloudy, and rainy spring has mirrored my heart and emotions, to the deepest part of my being. I speak the words as if God were having coffee with me: "Where is my husband, and why is he gone? We were married nearly thirty-five years, and now it's been almost eleven months since he's been gone. I'm now fifty-five years old, and after my busy years of being a wife and a mom who was all in, I now struggle to embrace this loneliness. This aloneness closes in on me like a dark silence in an unlit closet. How could my life have taken such a twisted turn away from the busy yet fun-loving bustle of marriage, family life, filled schedules, kids' games, family suppertime, vacations, and celebrations?"

I sense this still, small voice of Jesus saying to me, "I am always with you, and My Holy Spirit will comfort and guide you in the way you should go."

I seek the Lord's wisdom and discernment, His truth and direction. I still know God is with me and comforting me through this time, but I have so many unanswered questions. Where did I come from, and where am I going? What is my name, and why am I here?

I also hear God ask me, "What do you want Me to do for you, My dear child, and would you share your story?"

I don't know exactly how to answer Him, but I know I want to give meaning to these past years of my midlife and leave a legacy of truth to my children and my children's children. I pause to give my worries to God and pray the Lord's Prayer from Matthew 6:14 (KJV):

> Our father which art in heaven,
> hallowed be thy name.
> Thy kingdom come.
> Thy will be done, in earth,
> as it is in heaven.
> Give us this day our daily bread.
> And forgive us our debts,
> as we forgive our debtors.

And lead us not into temptation,
but deliver us from evil:
For thine is the kingdom, and the power,
and the glory,
for ever, and ever, Amen.

I pray through this time, I write through this time, and I lean in toward friends, family, and my Lord and Savior through this time of loss of what I once had. I lean into God's Word and my faith for a greater understanding of the pain and loneliness I'm currently going through. I still hope through the day, and I still dream at night with the stories and questions the Holy Spirit gives me to speak truth and direction into the unacknowledged desires and paths of my soul.

These are the truths and teachings from the NIV. (All verses, unless otherwise stated, are quoted from the New International Version of the Bible.)

When you walk, they will guide you;
when you sleep, they will watch over you;
when you awake, they will speak to you.
—Proverbs 6:22

Chapter 2

THE PRINCE AND
THE PROMISE

My diaries of dreams and desires contain every young girl's quest to be loved and to live her once-upon-a-time story in which she finds her handsome prince, and together they start a beautiful family and live happily ever after in their castle they call home. Her charming prince would be her hero, rescue her from her greatest fears, and fulfill her every passion for love, relationship, and family.

At the end of the day, her handsome prince would always come back to their castle. He'd be her provider, her hero, and her protector after coming back from slaying a dragon or two and conquering the enemy in battle. He would even make sure the boundaries of their kingdom and the castle walls were fortified and guarded so the evil queens and evil kingdoms couldn't penetrate their walled boundaries and plunder their home and family within. They would love each other forever and happily ever after.

The past days of childhood and the fairy-tale dreams of our perfect love stories with our families and our heroic knights in shining armor shift into the present, leading us to ask, "Now what?" We come face-to-face with the reality of our current times. The desires of love, family, home, and success remain the same, but the dreams of our best future and plans are interrupted by trials and tragedies that rock our current world and core foundation.

Our good plans for the future can dissipate like a fine gray mist, leaving us confused, shattered, and broken. This great interruption can leave us wanting to dump our entire past out the window, let go of our future dreams, and question how to live in this betwixt-and-between moment of now. These letters from my memoirs and journals, while under the cover of different names, are the true accounts of a woman, a wife, and a mother who desired the ideal life and love with her husband, Kevin, and her four beautiful daughters. This is my life, my testimony, and my message I leave behind in the form of letters and prayers of hope as a legacy of truth, love, and honor for generations to come.

August 1987

I lingered for a moment to look down at my beautiful bride's bouquet of peach roses, fragrant carnations, and pure white lilies. Tears welled up in my eyes as I lifted the perfect flowers to breathe in the fresh scent of roses. My mind was brought back to the day I went to my mom's room and sat on her bed to tell her about this wonderful guy I'd met named Kevin.

I recalled her words: "My dear, you are worthy of nothing less than the Prince Charming you've always dreamed about."

My misty-eyed gaze returned to the moment now before me as I readied myself to go down the church aisle. I wiped away the tears that were about to drop on my roses.

"What?" I asked my dad as I brought my mind back to a moment of clarity and the excitement of this day I'd anticipated for so long.

"Are you OK, girl?" he asked. "Do you not want to do this?"

"Oh, no," I replied. "Yes, I do! These are happy tears, Dad. I do want to do this."

"Well then, let's go. Just focus on the aisle, then look at the altar, and then look at him. Remember: aisle … altar … him; aisle … altar … him."

Dad and I quietly chuckled as he snuck in that fitting joke that pastors tell to break the ice just before reciting the wedding vows.

Pachelbel's "Canon" started playing, and I breathed in deeply. I was nervous. All eyes were on me, and I hoped I wouldn't trip on my gown. Excited, I anticipated the moment when I'd be right beside the love of my life and husband-to-be. Helena, my maid of honor and dear sister, straightened the long train of my silky, pure-white satin gown. After months of wrapping wedding cake in paper doilies, addressing invitations, and sewing coral satin bridesmaid dresses, everything and everyone was ready and seemed to be perfectly in place.

Dad was here by my side and ready to walk me down the aisle to meet my incredibly handsome groom. Kevin was wearing his striking black tuxedo and freshly pressed white shirt and gray tie. His blond hair gleamed under the sanctuary lights, and he stood ready to take my hand in marriage. For better or worse, for richer or poorer, in sickness and health, till death do us part. We couldn't wait to be married, and we wanted to proclaim our covenant promise and commitment to each other in the sanctuary before God and our friends and family. Our love and the joy of our promise reached all the way up to the courts of heaven that beautiful day in August.

Aside from the words the groomsmen had written on the bottom of Kevin's shoes that quietly shouted, "Save me," when we knelt to pray, and the decorations that were left on the reception room floor, everything was near-perfect that day.

> Love is patient, love is kind. It does not envy, it does not boast, it is not proud. It does not dishonor others, it is not self-seeking, it is not easily angered, it keeps no record of wrongs. Love does not delight in evil but rejoices with the truth. It always protects, always trusts, always hopes, always perseveres.
>
> —1 Corinthians 13:4–7

Chapter 3

THE NEW IDENTITY AND THE LOST-TEETH DREAM: 1987

These nighttime dreams wake me with a jolt from my slumber. Dreams become a metaphor to piece together the puzzle and questions that come from the reflection of my heart, soul, and mind. In the night, the Holy Spirit awakens my soul and reveals truth in stories and snapshots that shed light on the unacknowledged, dark nights of the soul. This dream awakened me to awareness of the new day.

I dreamed that I had a loose tooth, and it fell out. I woke up feeling like my tooth really had fallen out. The next week, I had a dream that the tooth beside my already lost tooth was loose, and it fell out as well. I woke up thinking I had really lost those couple of teeth.

The next week turned into the next month, and I continued the same dream, night after night for the entire year. The lost-teeth dream continually expanded from the previous dream that my teeth were falling out.

What is it about my teeth? Why am I continually dreaming about losing my teeth? I know this first year of marriage has been a year of changes, and becoming one with my husband had a few challenges. I acknowledge that this life-change and learning a new way of living together in marriage can be quite an adjustment, but why am I having these reoccurring dreams?

Every newly married couple faces change with this new reality and responsibility of becoming one, right? Gone are the selfish days of independence and the carefree attitude of single life. As I ponder and ask God for deeper meaning of this reoccurring dream, I hear the Holy Spirit speak truth in the meaning that my independent, carefree self was getting lost amongst the expectation of learning a new way to care for someone else and to learn how my new husband liked to do life. I learned that his underwear was supposed to be folded this way and not that way, his ironed shirts had to have just that right button closed before they were hung, all orderly, spaced, and by matching colors. I didn't mind this new world order of mine since I was a bit of a perfectionist myself, and I did strive to have everything in order and clean as well.

There are times, though, when I feel like I've lost my voice or ability to have an opinion. I feel like I've given up my voice, my identity, my smile, and my choice of the things I love. Kevin loved mayonnaise, so we bought that instead of the tangy Miracle Whip I liked and was used to. I didn't mind taking on his name, my new "Livingston" family name, although I had to think about writing it when I signed a check.

The computer was being used more in homes, and we'd record our home finances in a software program. I worked at a bank and took accounting classes in school, so I loved registering and calculating our budget and finances, but Kevin thought it best that he would now take over that role since he enjoyed the capabilities of discovering all the new home finance software for computers. I guess I didn't mind handing the financial responsibility over to him.

I thought about the reoccurring dream of losing my teeth. I proceeded to change the roll of toilet paper and switched it around, remembering Kevin liked it flipped over on top instead of under. Over was good, yet I felt like I was losing a bit of myself, and my smile was replaced with a questioning look of, "Is this okay? Is this the way you like it?" I'm sure the dream was alerting my soul to a few red flags that were to appear in the future as we continue this new, adventurous highway. Every individual experiences the loss of self in the first year of marriage, right?

Now, thirty-five years later, in 2022, I delve into my journals and reread the entries from my early years of being a wife. I wish I could go back in time and have a meaningful conversation with my younger self and maybe say this to her:

Dear Younger Me,

If I could go back in time, I'd visit you and share the deep understandings that I've learned through time and this truth with you. Your identity is not found in your husband or your family or the perfect and brilliant work you do, but your identity is found in Christ. God's given us our name and our voice, and in Him we will find meaning, we will find joy, and we will once again find our smile.

You were given the dream of losing your teeth because you were starting to lose your own identity and unique voice in Kevin's identity. God was trying to show you that you were losing a bit of yourself, your voice, your opinion, your choice, and your smile.

As the two of you become one flesh in marriage, please remember that you are still a complete, individual creation, designed with a purpose and free will. I know you need God's direction and the reassurance that your husband should love you for Whose you are and not for what you do for him or who your husband wants you to be. I know you need more time to get to know each of your unique parts, but don't lose your unique identity in Christ and who God created you to be. Don't deny all your own likes and your desires for your husband's ambitions, wants, and needs.

A wife joins union with her husband to be his help, his love, and his companion, but remember to leave room for Jesus to be your Savior and for the Holy Spirit to be your guide. Don't expect Kevin to lose himself in you, either. God designed you both to be one flesh, in marriage, and for keeping each other in a pure oneness, but you are both still individuals. Your unique identity in Christ will break forth to your destiny where your wholeness will bring your future into a purposeful completeness.

In the same way husbands ought to love their wives as their own bodies. He who loves his wife loves himself. After all, no one ever hated their own body, but they feed and care for their body, just as Christ does the church—for we are members of his body. For this reason a man will leave his father and mother and be united to his wife, and the two will become one flesh. This is a profound mystery—but I am talking about Christ and the church."

—Ephesians 5:28–32

So God created mankind in his own image, in the image of God he created them; male and female he created them.

—Genesis 1:27

Chapter 4

THE LIGHT THAT SHINES IN THE DARK: JUNE 2022

So many things make sense now as my new reality takes shape, but there are still so many questions left unanswered, and I cannot decipher if I am walking in God's greatest light of hope or merely stumbling through the darkness of the unknown. Maybe I will never know what has really happened and why we don't share our inner truths, only to sweep things under the mass carpet of denial. Time will tell.

I think back to my ongoing prayer through the years passed. I consider the exchanges of misunderstandings, miscommunication, and the confusion of not knowing the truth, and discovering lies and deception. I prayed the same prayer through the years: "Dear God, shine your light on the truth and expose the things that have gone on in the dark."

I hear His whisper in my heart, *I will be your light and your truth. Stay close to me and I will be your protector and your guide.*

Sometimes, God puts the flashlight of discovery in our hands, and we might be the only one in that dark closet to see and hear the truth. We may be the only ones there, the only one to come out of that hidden place of darkness and deception, the only one left holding the light, and the only one to be called to stand up for a cause and to be the voice to speak of those vulnerable and uncomfortable things for the sake of those who come behind us.

Now, what will we do once we know what we know, and once the truth becomes evident? Would we hide in the belly of the whale, afraid to expose the truth and avoiding the conviction of better judgment? Would we continue to conceal deception behind the mask of propriety to escape and hide from criticism and shame of our own past failures? No one wants to share the painful and hard truths, but this is my story; these are my private journals of my truth and God's call for me to be a voice that reaches generations to come and to say, "No, it's not all right. It's not all good. We must correct our behavior and get back into alignment with God's Word."

Would we dare to share our misgivings, disappointments, and disgraces so others will learn from our failures of boundaries crossed? I'll let you peek into my journals and secrets so all who come behind us, and the ones who have gone before us, will find us changed, transformed, repentant, forgiven, and faithful.

Will God find us hiding in our dark place and convict us to make a choice to come out of the dark closet of deception and disappointment? Will our good God find us cowering in our despair and gently remind us to have courage and come out into the light and back to Him? Yes, He will. He is the Good Shepherd, and He will leave the ninety-nine to find His one lost sheep. He will call His own back to restoration, and He will never leave us alone.

God is nudging us to choose to live a life with a greater purpose and leave a legacy of truth for all who walk behind us. Will we tell our children and grandchildren the truth so they can learn from our poor choices and decide to choose the higher ground of integrity and honor for our own family's sake? For Christ's sake? For Pete's sake?

Do we have to betray and discard the ones we love over and over to finally reclaim the truth, like Peter did, when he reaffirmed, three times over, "You know I love you, Lord." Are we nailing Jesus back on the cross repeatedly when we continue to walk in sin, when we call ourselves Christians?

God's calling us to be reconciled back to each other and back to the heavenly Father. Jesus Christ's severe mercy, all forgiving and redeeming love, is calling us back to His heart of grace, where healing comes in His Word and His truth.

Only pain and bitterness remain when we choose this chasm of dark separation and deep pain of division. God sees everything we do; we cannot run and hide from Him. When we turn and run back to God, we will find peace, for there is freedom in coming back into the light with repentance and forgiveness. There's blessing and joy on the horizon when we simply turn and pivot 180 degrees, repent, and choose the greater story and gift of redemption.

But whoever lives by the truth comes into the light, so that it may be seen plainly that what they have done has been done in the sight of God.

—John 3:21

Chapter 5

FINISHING WELL: 2022

I hear the interruption of my cell phone ring. It's Mom. Since my dad passed away five years ago, Mom is still embracing her new reality of being a widow and being alone. You would never know that she, as a widow of eighty-five years, still has some big questions: "Why? Who? And what on God's good earth has happened here?"

Somehow my mom, at the age of eighty-five, has been the epitome of an everyday saint. She still finds the energy and joy in a purpose while she looks after the old people and grows flowers in her garden to send home with anyone to brighten their day. Yesterday, she sent me home with three beautiful blooms of her first garden peonies. Mom, even though her back is now bent and stooped over, still drives and shops by herself; she still cleans and cooks for her family. She continually prays for us and reads children's Bible stories to her great-grandchildren, and she still calls me every day to encourage me with a poem or an incredibly applicable Bible verse. I miss my dad very much, but in this great loss of death, I am grateful my mom is still here for me.

My parents' stories are the ultimate version of real people finishing well amongst the struggles and hardships of life. Mom and Dad showed their love openly, and they weren't afraid to shout out a few words of discontent at one time or another, but they were real and honest, and I'm truly thankful to God for wise and discerning parents. They love, they care, and they pray for us even when we're not noticing. I also want to journey a life well-lived, with a purpose of leaving that same legacy of love, honor, integrity, and devotion to the ones we chose to love and the ones we're blessed to call family.

After I hang up my cell phone with Mom, I continue

reading my journal entries of my younger self and early experiences of being a wife and a mom. I decide to take a picture of one of my journal entries with my cell phone and share the images of these captured words with my dear family's group chat, which was once identified as "Team Livingston."

> We will not hide them from their descendants; we will tell the next generation the praiseworthy deeds of the Lord, his power, and the wonders he has done.
>
> —Psalm 78:4

> Praise the Lord. Blessed are those who fear the Lord, who find great delight in his commands. Their children will be mighty in the land; the generation of the upright will be blessed. Wealth and riches are in their houses, and their righteousness endures forever.
>
> —Psalm 112:1–3

Chapter 6

A LETTER FROM A MOTHER'S HEART

Journal Entry from March 1992

Today, I am so thankful to God and for you, my dear little daughter, Makenna Grace. You are now 17 months, almost a year and a half. I remember the day you were born on a beautiful autumn day in October. Your daddy was working the night shift, and I was alone counting the Braxton Hicks contractions and watching my big tummy cone up in a hard ball. This feeling was not painful, just a preparation for my body to bring you into the world. The contractions were consistent and ten minutes apart, so since your dad wasn't home, I tried leaving messages where he worked.

I wasn't successful in reaching your dad, so I decided to call your Auntie Helena, my only family in the city, to be with me. Auntie Helena came over, and we watched a cute Hallmark movie together.

At 11 a.m., the contractions were quite steady and becoming a bit more painful, so I decided to take a shower and get ready to go to the hospital. Well, that hot shower just made the pain more intense, and I called Auntie Helena to help me get ready.

She panicked as she tried to pull a brush through my long, blonde, wet hair and said, "Let's go, hurry up! We must leave for the hospital now."

I tried to stay calm and focused on my contractions and breathing when we got to the hospital. Kevin still wasn't at the hospital, and neither was my doctor. Finally, Kevin arrived, still in his work uniform, and got an update on my situation. At three centimeters dilation, they concluded I had a bit more time to still go through the contractions. I focused on my body's pain, my breathing, and the calming picture on the wall.

While I was in great pain yet trying to focus on the contractions and my breathing, your Auntie Helena and your Daddy were visiting on the couch. *Really?* I thought. I got super annoyed and wondered why my husband and my sister were having a conversation about a magazine article of the Cuban drug cartel. I was quite upset that my husband wasn't by my side, helping me through this painful process. This process called birthing was one of the miracles of life, and it was happening right now.

No one believed me when I cried out, "I have to push now!"

The nurses said I was a long way off, but then I shouted, "No! The baby is coming now!"

The nurses checked and said, "Yes, she's fully dilated; call the doctor now!"

Within five minutes and three pushes, there you were, Makenna, our precious miracle. The doctor barely got his scrubs tied on in time to catch you. The entire process, from arriving at the hospital to having to push, took only one hour. You came into our lives without much struggle and a bright twinkle in your eyes.

The first night you came home, I was alone with

you. Your Dad couldn't take the time off work to be home with me and you. It was a tough night being home alone with you on that first night, but it was a special time to be able to bond with you. This great big love, wrapped in a tiny bundle, finally came to me as you, my newborn, with your big navy-blue eyes peering past your little nightcap and your tiny finger clinging to mine. That was a tough night, though.

My milk hadn't set in yet, and you were so upset and hungry. I never thought I would need any infant formula and thought I would be breastfeeding just fine. There was nothing that calmed you, and I was so distraught to hear you cry. I noticed the music box that I used to play you when you were still in my tummy. You heard that music and stopped crying and stared up into my eyes as the comforting sound calmed your cry. That music and my mom's long-distance call suggesting that I should put some boiled water with a touch of sugar, into an infant bottle to feed you, calmed you right down, and we were both content to finally fall asleep.

In the morning, although your dad was extremely tired from working the night shift, he was so overjoyed to hold his new baby girl, and we cuddled in bed with you as we marveled at how adorable and tiny you were. We had to be careful, because it was too easy and comfortable to fall asleep while holding you on our chest. You loved the comfort of falling asleep to the motion and sound of our breath and beating heart.

Makenna, your hair is so soft and curly and frames your cherub-like face and big blue-green eyes. Now, 17 months later, some people say that you look a little more like your mommy. What a gift and an honor it is to be your mom.

You bring true joy to your mommy and daddy's life, and you help us to stop and realize the important things in our world. You have a good attention span, which allows you to learn so quickly. You mimic us with your words and actions, and now you're really into trying on my high-heeled shoes. You, my dear Makenna, are reaching some milestones right now. You don't depend on your bottle for nighttime, and you tell us when you need to go potty, although you don't always get there in time.

Your mamma's thoughts today are full of excitement. Your mommy and daddy are going to find out if we bought our first new home today! I feel a bit anxious about this, and we have had to learn how to be patient and trust that God will help us make it through our financial worries.

I feel excited about being in a larger, and newer, three-bedroom home to call our own. Since we've lived in the small townhouse at student housing, your Daddy had to share his study with you in your baby nursery. We were a little cramped, and this new home will give us room to grow. We are so blessed and thankful that your grandpa could help us with a down payment for our new home. I would still be content if our home purchase didn't go through since I've had to quit my job and then your Daddy wouldn't have to work as hard. Mommy misses Daddy when he's always at school in the day and working the night shift. It's hard finding balance with family, work, school, and finances, but whatever happens, I know that God will provide for us, and our Lord will help our family overcome anything when we put our trust in Him.

> Husbands, in the same way be considerate as you live with your wives, and treat them with respect as the weaker partner and as heirs with you of the gracious gift of life, so that nothing will hinder your prayers.
>
> —1 Peter 3:7

Chapter 7

THE SHABBY AND
THE CHIC

November 1992

There is a picture I love so dearly. It portrays my feelings
so well today. It's a Robert Duncan painting of a young
mom holding her baby in her white cotton, nightgown,
expressing a bit of sadness while looking out the window.
I see in her eyes a melancholy, lonely, but peaceful feeling
as she looks out the window, wondering what life had
to offer beyond the four walls of motherhood. It's as
though she is waiting for her only physical connection
to the outside world, her husband, to come home.

The young mom in this picture wears her hair plainly pulled back, and her nightgown is made of pure white cotton, with gatherings that hide her motherly figure. She holds her baby in a lovingly close but exhausted way. Oh, how I can relate to her, this mom who's portrayed in the picture that hangs on my bathroom wall.

I remember back to 1990, when Makenna was a newborn. One morning, I finally got her back to sleep after nursing and changing her. I went down to the kitchen, in my nightgown, for a glass of water. When I got down to the foot of the stairs to the family room, I noticed there was a stranger in the room. She was a pretty, young girl, all dressed up, sitting on my couch.

I was shocked and puzzled and embarrassed all at the same time. I gasped and started to turn around to run back upstairs, but then I realized this was my house, and why was this strange girl sitting on my couch in my family room? What?

Quickly, I turned back around on my heel, looked at her, and asked, "Who are you, and why are you here in my home?"

"Oh, I'm just waiting for Kevin. He told me to go inside and wait for him while he warms the car. Sorry, I didn't know … ah, Kevin invited me to drive together with him to class. Oh, well, I'll go back outside now; the car should be warm by now anyway."

My mind was reeling with questions: *Who in the world was this strange woman in my family room on my couch, and why on earth did Kevin not forewarn me that someone, another woman, was in my home? Did he think I was sleeping and would never know? Oh, my word.*

My heart was pounding inside my chest. I was so upset and embarrassed; I felt intruded upon and disrespected. I will admit I was jealous that this young, pretty, and very well-dressed girl was going to be driving in the same car and spending time in class together with my husband.

Here I was, baby mamma, all disheveled from waking up five times through the night to nurse our newborn, in my shabby nightgown and morning robe. I can still barely recall the days before we had a baby, the days just outside these four walls of wifely duty and motherhood. I can still remember how I used to get all dressed up in chic suits, to go to work in a professional, downtown atmosphere. Those days seemed like just yesterday, and yet they are a fading memory disappearing like the gray mist on a cloudy day.

Dear Younger Me,

You've experienced so much with your husband together as new parents, and you've also had to manage a lot on your own. Your husband was working hard and going to university to provide for his family, but you didn't see the red flags that were warning you to share your struggles with him. A husband needs to understand that now that you're married, you both need to communicate your feelings and discuss those boundaries that both of you should respect. When your husband let another woman enter your home without you knowing, that was disrespectful and inconsiderate. I know you felt a huge intrusion to find this strange woman in your home.

Instead of sharing this experience, you swept your hurts and feelings under the carpet of chores, duty, and sleepless nights. Those were difficult days for both of you, and I know you needed him to be more present during the birthing process and to be by your side to share and help in the fatherly role.

You missed those days of getting dressed in classy, professional clothes and having a career.

I know you longed to spend more time doing something fun with Kevin, where your hearts and minds could connect in shared dreams, goals, and pursuits. Your feelings were valid. You are not a nobody who just cares for the home and the family; you are an intelligent and beautiful woman. You are a caring and loving mom who wants to be present for your husband and new baby.

You were taught, with regard to your former way of life, to put off your old self, which is being corrupted by its deceitful desires; to be made new in the attitude of your minds; and to put on the new self, created to be like God in true righteousness and holiness.

—Ephesians 4:22–24

She is clothed with strength and dignity; she can laugh at the days to come. She speaks with wisdom, and faithful instruction is on her tongue.

She watches over the affairs of her household and does not eat the bread of idleness.

Her children arise and call her blessed; her husband also, and he praises her:

"Many women do noble things, but you surpass them all."

Charm is deceptive, and beauty is fleeting; but a woman who fears the Lord is to be praised.

Honor her for all that her hands have done, and let her works bring her praise at the city gate.

—Proverbs 31:25–31

Chapter 8

DOUBLE JOY

June 1992

There are so many wonderful blessings to thank God for. Our precious second daughter arrived in the beautiful month of June 1992. Brooklyn Joy Livingston came as a gift from God into our lives, and she was a content, six-pound, eleven ounce, and 19.5-inch bundle of blessing.

That Monday night we had our friends over with their young toddler, who was the same age as Makenna. We cooked a wonderful barbecue dinner together, but as soon as we sat down to eat, I started to have some uncomfortable contractions. The excitement began, and supper was cut short.

Kevin and I arrived at the hospital at 8:00 p.m., and our second, beautiful baby girl arrived, with a mound of hair, at 11:30 p.m. The entire labor was about three and a half hours, a little longer than with Makenna, but once the doctor broke my water, our new baby was ready to push through into this brave new world. The bonding was wonderful, and I was so aware and able to enjoy my precious, new baby.

The hospital stay was enjoyable and restful since I had a room to myself. The view through the window was beautiful on that first day of summer, as boats sailed by on the river as the backdrop, and the mountains framed the river and green golf course.

Brooklyn, my sweet baby, you are so calm, and I watch you bond easily with me in this miraculous connection called life, love, and nurture. What a miracle of life you are to me! You nurse so naturally, and you're so adaptive that you even take the bottle well. You hardly cry, and you're calmed by just a few words or a cuddle. Your new life is such a blessing and a miracle to us, and even as I feel my uterus contract like a painful memory of the birthing process, I think we must have more of these tiny miracles in the future. Brooklyn, I call you my Gemstone, and you are adorable with so much soft, blonde hair, a cute heart-shaped face, long piano fingers like Makenna's, and even your beautiful bow lips are like your sister's.

Makenna is a super sister with her new baby Brooki. She is so gentle when she strokes your hair, hugs you, and holds your hand, yet she can't understand why you won't hold the toys and why you don't want the stuffed animals piled high on top of you.

Grandma is here to help for a few days, and Makenna loves it. She always enjoys all the hugs and kisses she can get, especially from Daddy. I think Makenna has been gifted at learning fast at this stage. She is twenty months old and talks so well that many people are impressed. Maybe that's every proud mamma's point of view. She is our petite little angel with the most gorgeous curly, blonde hair. At least she looks like an angel. Since she's having to adapt to sharing her time with a new sister; her angelic self tends to be a bit jealous and cranky. Yet, I love how Makenna can be found hugging her baby Brook or sitting on her teddy bears, reading books over and over and wanting to play with the "bubbos" while Mommy washes the dishes.

> Behold, children are a heritage from the
> Lord, offspring a reward from him.
>
> —Psalm 127:3

Chapter 9

A BEAUTIFUL MESS

September 1992

I thought that writing in my diaries would prevent me from going insane. I tried to talk with an adult, but no one would answer my phone calls. Things are hectic around here. I'm providing daycare for a few friends and neighbors' children by looking after two other children to help with our family's income. Life is a little bit unpredictable right now with four toddlers and babies under the age of two years. Lunches and snacks dropping on the ground, dirty diapers, runny noses, fighting over toys, lipstick on the carpet, and bed-wetting is really getting me down.

I am so exhausted. Thank goodness that my girlfriend finally just called me. What a much-needed change of topic to just simply have conversation with another adult. I've really searched my heart lately.

I've been praying to God that I can cope with these testing years of looking after toddlers and babies, and that I can just make it through the day. The number-one priority on the to-do list today is, keep the tiny humans alive.

Makenna has been pushing her limits in so many ways and does not listen until I either yell at her or follow through with the discipline I keep promising. I think she wants more of my full-time attention and her alone time with Mommy. I get that; who wouldn't want more alone time with Mommy? I want more alone time with Mommy! I'm sure that Daddy wants more alone time with Mommy.

These years of looking after a two-year-old and a newborn are very testing times. Makenna, at the age of two, wants to do so much on her own, yet she can't quite do things without making messes and saying, "No!" or asking, "Why?" Makenna is an extreme child.

I mean, when she is good, she is incredibly good, and she is excellent at learning, but when she acts out of frustration and jealousy, she is extremely good at that too. Whatever Makenna puts her mind to in life, she will do very well.

When Makenna grows up, I don't think she will settle for mediocre. She is going to want a whole lot of spicy creativity, and she will excel in whatever she wants to do. It is my job to direct her energy and vigor into a good, godly, and right direction. God help me do this and help me be a good mother who knows the right way to discipline in love.

I would not exchange these young, stay-home mamma days, although tiresome, for the highest paid position in a large firm downtown. I will acknowledge that these baby years are too precious and pass by way too quickly. I want to be there for my baby's first smile, her first steps, and the first time she says, "Mamma." Why is it, though, that their first word is usually "Dadda"? Dadda is hardly around these days.

Brooklyn is growing far too fast. Time seems to slip by too quickly with a second child. At night, when I hold her and nurse her, I wish I could capture the moment so I could bring it back when I am fifty. I hope that all these journal entries I write and pictures I take will someday capture the moments that we can't replace. I hope that these words can somehow be a time capsule to remember the warmth and satisfaction I feel while cradling, nursing, and bonding with my baby.

Dear Younger Me,

Now that I'm fifty-five, and I reread your words, my words, from my journals, from so many years ago, I know you have a pure desire to be the best mom and wife you can be, and you want to be present to experience those most precious years with your treasured family. I know the days of being a young mom can be overwhelming and so very tiresome. I know that you and Kevin desire to be good parents, who love and discipline and teach their children well. I remember that you both took your role as parents seriously and responsibly. Be encouraged; you were and are loving parents. You were a very loving wife, a good mom, and a good homemaker.

Your bond with your sweet children will grow into a beautiful, lifelong relationship, and God will give you strength, peace, and provision for this challenging new journey of parenthood.

When you get tired, frustrated, and anxious, remember your little ones are a blessing from God, and He will guide you. You will be blessed because you taught your children the promises in the Bible.

You took the time to love your children, and after you fed them and bathed them, you read to them every night; you tucked them in their safe, clean, and comfy beds with a song, a kiss, and a prayer. Your children will remember those things you taught them. That was the cherished living legacy that your mother passed down to you and that you are now passing down to your children. Your children will remember how you loved them.

You will see the fruit of those loving, caring times, and those teachings that you planted like seeds deep inside them. One day, those seeds will burst forth into new life, when your children will have their own children. They will remember, I promise you that! Even if it's only because they are reading your heart here in these words that you leave behind for them. These words and these truths will not go unheard without leaving an impression on their hearts.

October 1992

Brooklyn, you reached another milestone today. You giggled once on September 1, and the other day, I was overjoyed to laugh with you for the first time. I wish your Daddy was here more to experience that with you. You are so aware of your family these days. If anyone walked into our family room right now, they would find Makenna trying to sit on you and hug you, her baby sister, "Brooki," and Makenna would be dancing to music like a little galloping pony with a Tupperware bowl on her head.

Makenna says everything these days, but her favorite line is, "I sleeping," when I'm trying to get her to eat. These days, she knows when we are approaching our home by the lake, and before we reach our house, she often reminds us to get the mail.

My wish for my girls is that you will grow up to love God and be happy and successful in everything you do. May God keep you healthy, and may He assign special angels to keep watch over you. If I could freeze time in a bottle, I'd capture this moment and seal it away for all time to remember this moment. My children, you keep me smiling and bring so much joy to me. I love you girls and thank God for you every day. I know that your dad wishes he could see you more, and I wonder what he's doing today as he goes to university and then goes to work his night shift work. He is one busy man trying to do it all. I miss him so very much.

> Come to me, all you who are weary and burdened, and I will give you rest. Take my yoke upon you and learn from me, for I am gentle and humble in heart, and you will find rest for your souls. For my yoke is easy and my burden is light.
>
> —Matthew 11:28–30

> These commandments that I give you today are to be on your hearts. Impress them on your children. Talk about them when you sit at home and when you walk along the road, when you lie down and when you get up. Tie them as symbols on your hands and bind them on your foreheads. Write them on the doorframes of your houses and on your gates.
>
> —Deuteronomy 6:6–9

Chapter 10

FOR THE LOVE OF FAMILY

January 1993

Kevin is now twenty-seven years old and finishing off his fourth year of university and desperately trying to get good grades. Being a stay-at-home mom of two toddlers is challenging, and the expectation of family life has hit us both in the face like a wet washcloth on a sleepy morning.

Kevin's been going to the gym and working out and doing independent lab studies and research at the university. He's either at work or at school or needing me to keep the house quiet while he sleeps. That's not easy to do with two toddlers underfoot. He's been on a diet and lost twenty pounds and decided to change his hair to the side, and I think it looks rather dashing on him.

I'm feeling old and run-down at the age of twenty-six. It's challenging looking after two little ones and being pregnant again with our third baby. The only thing that greets me in the morning is the toilet bowl as I nauseously run to the great throne of mercy. Unending morning sickness is the cross I've had to bear in exchange for quick, painkiller-free, natural births. I'm happy to be having another sweet baby, and I'm mostly content with being a stay-home Mom.

I do wish that I could go on a date or a vacation, or celebrate Valentine's with Kevin, but his work and studies are consuming all his time. Thank goodness for Ladies Time Out at church. It's not really a time-out break since I have to get the two little ones out of the house by 9 a.m. and gather craft supplies, Bible study notes, and snacks, but it's imperative that I connect with other ladies and young moms. What would I do without the support of the church?

I want to challenge myself by learning new things

so that I don't get stagnant and depressed. I'd love to get my floral design diploma and bookkeeping diploma, but I can't quite seem to find the strength and time to get all the housework and laundry done while the children nap. I cannot wait until spring when we can get out in the yard, grow some grass, plant some flowers, and build a fence to keep the dogs out and the kids safe inside our yard. There are many dreams of home projects we want to do and drapes I'd like to put up in our new home, but money is tight, and paying student loans off is still an ongoing priority.

> But those who hope in the Lord will renew
> their strength. They will soar on wings
> like eagles; they will run and not grow
> weary, they will walk and not be faint.
> —Isaiah 40:31

Chapter 11

THE THIRD THRILL

September 1993

There's going to be another baby in the house. I am looking forward to all the fun experiences our new baby and our little family will bring us. I thank God for His continued protection over us and the many wonderful things life brings. Being a wife and stay-home mommy is keeping me remarkably busy. Some days, I think it would be easier to put the kids in daycare and go back to work, but the cost would be too great on so many levels. There needs to be at least one parent present with the children. Maybe one day, I'll be able to start a new home-based business so I can still stay home with my children and help pay for a few expenses, so their daddy doesn't have to work as hard as he does.

It was a nice summer, although the Alberta summers are too short and too cool for my liking. It's now September, and some of my flowers that I started by seed, under my kitchen window, are now outside and taking root but haven't even bloomed yet. The frost has now hit the flowers prematurely and stolen any hope for them to bloom.

We went back to our old hometown for your daddy's ten-year high-school reunion and a family wedding. Kevin has been enjoying the summer off with not enough work, but it gives him time to study for finals.

Last week, some interesting changes happened. Our new truck was stolen and totaled, and we sold our other two cars. It all worked out good financially, and now we have a new sports car. Daddy sure loves that Toyota Supra, MK4, but I still drive the mini-van with the kids in car seats. Sometimes I ask myself what it would it be like to drive around in a new sports car again, just like when I was young and single, driving my bright red Corvette.

January 1994

Never a dull moment in the Livingston household. We are now the proud parents of our third beautiful daughter. Everleigh Hope was born on an icy day in January 1994, at 11:30 a.m. She weighed eight pounds, five ounces, and measured twenty-one inches long. She is such a beautiful baby girl and has some features like her sisters. She smiles already and can have a loud cry when she wants to. Her hair feels like satin down, and I am amazed at how soft her skin feels. Welcome to our family, sweet baby girl, and I pray that with God's help, we will raise you up in a loving Christian family. We love you so much, baby Everleigh.

Makenna is such a good mommy at three years old. She introduces Everleigh as her baby. She makes us proud that she is so gentle and wants to nurse her new little baby, just like Mommy. We have to watch her, though, for today I caught her carrying Everleigh around. Sometimes, I am saddened that Makenna must grow up too fast and that we expect so much from her. Maybe too much? She still wants to be a baby sometimes and asks for a little baby bottle too and at times wants us to spoon-feed her like her younger sister, Brooklyn.

Brooklyn, our little gem, also must grow up too fast. She makes us proud of how gentle she is with her new baby sister. She strokes baby Everleigh's hair so gently and giggles after giving her a soft kiss on the head.

After the kiss, she laughs and says, "Fuzzy!" I hope I can remember the song in her voice and the way she excitedly says, "Look, look, looook!"

She loves her blanket, and I love the way she sucks a corner of the blanket ever so calmly. Brooklyn, like Makenna, is very sensitive, but I think Brooklyn can show her sensitivity more, and now at the age of one and a half, she is starting to show her individual will and independence. She now loves to do everything by herself.

I love the way the girls run to the door when Daddy comes home and to see them run around and squeal with delight just makes my heart melt. I miss him so much too when he goes to work and to university. Brooklyn has a funny way of saying, "Hello Daddy," with her growly, singing voice. I pray that I can give all my girls the attention they need in these busy, early years, and I long to have more time alone with Kevin, including going on dates with him.

We are still living in our lovely, newer home by

the lake, but the next six months should prove to be interesting. Now that Kevin has finally graduated from university, I'm sure glad to have my husband home more. We needed time together as a family, and it's such a relief to finally have an income to help pay the bills.

I don't have much of a life outside of these four walls of motherhood, but I am trying to complete my floral design diploma through correspondence while the kids nap, and I still anxiously await the results of my book publication offers. I have many doubts, but I hope that somehow, someday, I can make that little dream come true.

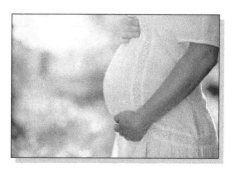

My Ray of Sunshine

Mothers often want to forget the pains of birth, but I want to remember how our little girls came into the world. My pregnancy with Everleigh seemed to be too long; she was a week overdue. I think she was too cozy inside and didn't want to come out into the freezing, January winter in Alberta. It was quite a different and uncomfortable pregnancy, so we thought she would be a little boy.

I was lucky to have my water break that Friday morning at 8:00 a.m.; it was a cold January morning, and I don't think I would have made it to the hospital in time. I had so many Braxton contractions the last two months that I thought I would have the baby every night. At 9:30 a.m., Kevin and I went to the hospital, while Auntie Helena came over to look after the girls. I had no heavy contractions to speak of, so I thought the birth would drag on for a long time. So I thought.

I was very fortunate to have textbook, speedy deliveries. The delivery doctor knew I had quick and uncomplicated deliveries, so he asked me if some obstetric med students could view my birth and learn from the experience. By the third baby, all dignity flies out the window, and since there's no concealing what's really behind the white sheet of the birthing process, I agreed.

The students might as well learn and see what really happens in this beautiful mess of birth, so the whole crew of students came to view my birthing process. Between unashamed, excruciating pushes, I felt like a specimen under the microscope. The team of medical students "ooh'd" and "aah'd" as they crouched down and peered in with scrunched faces, as if they were experiencing the process right alongside me. They kind of looked like umpires crouching behind the batter. Well, I've come to accept the unashamed and full disclosure of life's painful and messy experiences.

At 10:30 a.m., I felt an internal change, as those ever-familiar contractions kicked in. I had a few very intense contractions and about five hard pushes, and an hour later, there she was. Our little, lovely, baby Everleigh was born, and although it was freezing winter outside, she came into our world like a ray of sunshine that warmed our hearts. Thank God the birth wasn't any longer because without any painkillers or spinal blocks, I was totally aware of the pain and too totally aware of the cheering squad of med students. My quick deliveries made up for the months and months of morning sickness and vomiting.

When I'm old and gray, and sit with Kevin, waiting for our children to phone home, I hope these letters will bring back some good memories. It's good to remember the hardships and the painful times that come through the birthing process, to remember the tears, to remember the laughter, and most of all, to remember our love.

> My frame was not hidden from you when
> I was made in the secret place, when I was
> woven together in the depths of the earth.
> Your eyes saw my unformed body; all the
> days ordained for me were written in your
> book before one of them came to be.
>
> —Psalm 139:15–16

Chapter 12

THE DEGREES OF LOVE, PURSUITS, AND FAMILY: MARCH 1995

I finally completed my floral design course. Flowers, to me, are the eighth wonder of the world. Just like a child is a miraculous gift from God, so are flowers. The poetry that comes from the beauty of a flower makes my senses tingle. I have many dreams to finally be debt-free and able to enjoy time with my husband and children on an acreage. My secret fantasy is to be surrounded by flowers I have started by seed. I am not sure if I will ever work in this field, but I know that floral design and horticulture will always fascinate me.

The past year of 1994 was also a year to discover myself and to tell myself I can do anything I put my mind to, with God's help. I have so many joys, and the anticipation of discovering more of the brilliance of life reminds me that I can't do it all, at least not all at once, and I must prioritize my life and my pursuits. I must be selective to put my mind on the appropriate things that call to my attention in this season of life.

I have discovered the joy in floral design, in writing, and even in painting. I know I am not outstanding in any field, but experimenting is helping me to discover my true gifts and help me enjoy a few other things in life than just being a wife and mom. I shouldn't say "just" being a wife and mom, because some of our greatest callings come through the everyday, commonplace duties in a family. Yet I struggle with the desires of learning more, giving up a university degree, and fulfilling the calls within my heart as a wife and a mom.

I strive to be the perfect wife, the ideal mom, and I struggle with the idea of being faultless, even in my creativity of painting and writing. I fear the opinions others have of me, and I fear criticism, ridicule, and rejection. For now, my greatest passion is for my family, to make a loving environment in my home and a sanctuary of peace for my husband to come home to.

Kevin and I are in our sixth year of marriage, and our love has flourished now that he's only been working and not going to university. He's been around for me and the girls a bit more, and we've been able to express our passion for each other more throughout each day. There has been a new side to Kevin, which he's been hiding for a while.

His complimentary way has been coming out and dazzling my senses back to life. I love it and am reminded of the great love I have for him. He was my first true love, and there are real butterfly feelings in my tummy that I still get when he kisses me. I've never had those deep feelings for anyone else. These mysterious butterflies I feel in my tummy flutter by unannounced, like a surprise, even when I recall a special moment with him.

Along with the butterflies, I've felt a suspended dizziness that comes over me like a mystical potion. This intimate connection is my truest expression of love for him. I am so blessed to share my life with him and to have him around to share more time with our children and to share not just the depth of our physical love, but our everyday considerations of love.

There is a mysterious side to Kevin, though, and I think back to when we first met. He said something quite frankly and curious when he made the comment, "You'll never really know me." I've always wondered why he said that. It's my personal pursuit to know him and understand him better, since I believe that is where true intimacy lies; it's in the knowing. I think I know this man I married.

Kevin seems to be in search for something bigger, better, faster, and smarter, other than a wife and family, which I think we're quite enough for him. He pursues excellence and higher education. I am saddened, though, to see him struggle to be someone greater and to want to hang more degrees on the wall, even if he'll never say it out loud. I see that in him. I hope we finally arrive at contentment and peace with love, life, and family. We have so much to be grateful for as we are.

Kevin's father often said he could have gone so much further in life and business if he would have just had more education. Those words, to know more, seem to be the unspoken challenge and competition in pursuit of the greatest of men. The insatiable desire for meaning and purpose all too often translates into a dare for greatness, power, and the quest for more. Some think that the more you have, the happier you will be. The desires of the unquenched heart often make us put on the invisible boxing gloves that taunt, "Bring it on."

I don't think two strong-willed men can rule in the same household. There must finally be a day of reckoning with who's really in control and who's the head of the household. There's a careful balance in the father-son role after the son moves out and marries and has children of his own. Men need to be king of their own castle, and there's nothing wrong with that.

I respect the man who is under the authority of God and realizes he has an honorable role as the head of the family. I also see there can be a great struggle with fathers and sons becoming boys to men. There is a situational difference between the "obey" of childhood to the "honor" of the adult son to a father. A child needs to obey the wishes and teachings of a good and wise parent, and a grown and married son should be wise enough to make his own decisions, to lead his own family, while still showing respect and honor towards his father. I believe every son wants to hear his father say, "Well done, my son, good job."

The Livingston family lived a highly productive and successful life, knowing they could accomplish great things, and they knew their reward would be to have more, know more, and get more, bigger, better, and newer things. If one was good, then two were better. Their modus operandi was "Anything you can do, I can do better. What they don't know won't hurt them. I'll scratch your back if you scratch my back, and just get rid of it if it no longer serves you."

As Livingstons, we were taught to enjoy the fruits and rewards of our labor, especially in favorable times. It was common to buy more and sell higher, or trade in something old and buy something bigger, better, and newer. If Livingstons liked a new shirt, they'd get one in red and yellow and black and white. Kevin learned the same thing, and why not? This was the pursuit of happiness and bigger things to come. There's nothing wrong with getting ahead in life; I agree to some degree, but at what expense? One must stop and consider when enough is enough.

The Livingstons were generous people, especially when it was legal to exchange a government tax payment for a worthy mission deduction. They always cared for their own family bloodline and helped with open hands, wherever it was beneficial. They were discreet in their sharing, and they had good intentions.

Kevin had an excellent mind and desired to help, to be a hero. He was smarter, stronger, and more charming than most, and in my mind, he was on his way to be an outstanding problem-solver to anyone who needed him and consulted in him. He was energized and motivated in praise and finished the goals on his checklist. Kevin knew what he wanted to accomplish in life, and he challenged himself to know more and be the best at whatever he set out to do. Those who were lucky enough to rub shoulders with him felt honored; they were eager to be around him and hear more of what he had to say and what he could teach them. He had book smarts, street smarts, strength, authority, charm, and charisma, and he was destined to be a great man.

Now, Kevin's talking about going back to school again to get his master's degree. The idea of him going back to school scares me a little, but I don't want to tell him what he can or shouldn't do. I long to find some normalcy and peace in contentment of a regular family, where the husband has a decent career, brings home a paycheck, and spends time with his family on the weekends. Going back to school when we just had our third baby means less money and less time with him as a wife and as parents to our family.

Wherever we go, whatever we do, I hope our goal is to prioritize our God, our own family, and still pursue each other in love and marriage. Together, we will experience many happy family times together.

Dear Younger Me,

You've always embraced the bonds of relationship and family, and you appreciated that there was more to life than having a bigger house and a newer car. You experienced the stress on your family and the challenges of the continual pursuit of wanting and obtaining more. Your husband wanted to please his father and you all by getting more for his family. God only knows our heart, and He knows our motives.

God will supply your needs. Wake up, take note, and be discerning of what is important in life. Do not worry. God is your provider. Sit down with Kevin, and take a moment to reflect on how you might balance your relationship and your extended family with your career goals and life choices.

But store up for yourselves treasures in heaven, where moths and vermin do not destroy, and where thieves do not break in and steal. For where your treasure is, there your heart will be also.

—Matthew 6:20–21

Chapter 13

WHEN THE CAT'S AWAY, THE MICE WILL PLAY

August 1995

Everleigh has been running almost at the same time as she started to walk, around fourteen months. She often gets knocked down by her sisters, but before she gets discouraged and frustrated, she somehow manages to get back up, shake off the tears, and run after her sisters again and again, in sheer determination.

Her determination reminds me of the words in that

song by Chumbawamba, "I get knocked down, but I get up again." She laughs and smiles a lot and tends to whine when she's exhausted and hungry. Who doesn't whine when they're exhausted and hungry? She's just like her mamma and even her daddy. We can all get hangry sometimes. We're all just trying to survive and keep up with the day-to-day activities of life. Everleigh now has twelve teeth and loves to eat, and she grows leaps and bounds with each bite of food and bounce of joy. Her hair is like sheer-spun, white gold and sweeps into her green-blue eyes. She loves being part of the gang, and now that we can go outside to play, she loves adventures on the swing and alligator teeter-totter in our back yard.

We love to get out as a family and go to the zoo on the weekends when Kevin is around and when we're able to steal a few hours away from his studies. Kevin couldn't get away from his work and studies too often, so he encouraged me to take the three girls and journey from Alberta to British Columbia to visit Oma and Opa, my mom and dad.

A seven-hour road trip to British Columbia alone with three little girls was a bit challenging, but we became accustomed to managing without Kevin. We then continued, with my parents, for another twenty-hour drive in their motorhome to attend my cousin's wedding in California. What a fun adventure that was, and I wish that Kevin was able to go with us, but he had to work and get ready to start university again. I am so sad to have to do most of my life alone with the kids and not be able to enjoy many family vacations together.

The kids and I had a great time, making memories with Oma and Opa on that trip to California. We experienced the huge trees of the redwood forest, picked up shells and driftwood by the ocean shore, and all the other fun times that come with a family wedding and keeping up with three little ones.

Yesterday, we were visiting with the parents of the bride; Everleigh got so excited to run after her sisters and followed them out the back door of the house. Being just a toddler, Everleigh didn't realize the screen door shut behind Brooklyn, and she ran right into the screen door and took the entire door down. It would've been hilarious if I hadn't felt so horribly embarrassed. The bride's family was all so very nice and gracious as they set the door aside to fix it later. Oh man, what a trip.

I'm not going to lie: My dad's overly confident driving in the motorhome on the winding and narrow cliffside roads of Highway 101 and the streets of San Francisco absolutely frightened me.

I was glad to be home and welcomed the collegiate feeling of the cool and fresh air that September in 1995 brought with it.

The Bull and Ringmaster Dream

What was that dream all about? I questioned myself, trying to remember the details that unfolded upon waking early that morning. Kevin had already gone to school, and I lingered in bed for a moment to consider my dream. In the dream, just moments before waking, I was in a large stadium or arena, with hundreds of people seated around watching the ringmaster, waving his cape of red.

"Are you all ready for a mighty show and demonstration of courage?" he shouted out to the cheering crowd. "Who will take on this mighty bull?"

Everyone cheered and shouted, yet no one volunteered. He had a basket full of snakes and rats that the ringmaster threw far into the crowd seated in the stadium. Somehow all those snakes and rats flew in my direction and landed on me.

Much to my horror, the ringmaster pointed to me and shouted, "You, come down here to the center ring."

I was terrified and overwhelmingly afraid as I was suddenly transported into the middle of the stadium. The bull stared me down. His nostrils snorted and flared as his hoof stomped angrily, ready to charge me.

The ringmaster came to where I sat, cowering, in the middle of the ring. He took a rod he held in his hand and proceeded to draw a circle around me in the sand. He told me to sit in the middle of the circle he drew in the sand and told me not to go outside of the ring. I was terrified, but I did what he said.

The bull charged me in angry fury and then stopped just before the ring around me. The bull ran around the ring and furiously charged me again, but again just stopping short of the circle the ringmaster put me in.

I gasped in fear and woke up with eyes wide open. I breathed deeply and remembered how I trembled in a cowering position. I was safe, hiding my face, on my knees, in the middle of the ring. Even though I was terrified, I was continually safe when I stayed in the middle of the circle the ringmaster drew around me.

I pondered my dream as I unpacked my suitcase from the long road trip. I put away a pile of freshly folded laundry into the girls' bedroom drawers and thought about the dream with the bull and me in the ringmaster's circle. I considered the thought that I might be heading into something frightening and bigger than myself. This dream seemed to be warning me that something was coming that would be bigger than what I could manage on my own, or maybe I just ate something bad for supper last night. Like in my dream, I went on my knees and prayed; I gave my fears to God and asked for protection in the days ahead. I had no idea at that time why I had dreamed this dream, but the truth of it came to light in the next couple of days.

The girls were down for a nap now, and I thought it would be a perfect, undisturbed moment to clean the master bathroom. As I washed the floor, I thought about how much I missed Kevin these days, especially when he wanted me to vacation with the girls by myself. I didn't want to go without him, and I wished we could spend more time together.

I thought more and continued to wash the bathroom floor. As I scrubbed the floor, I noticed something. I pulled a long, dark hair from the cloth. I was puzzled and wondered why there was a long dark hair on my bathroom floor, when the girls and I had shorter blonde hair. I didn't know anyone with long dark hair who would have been in my bathroom.

This disturbed me quite a bit since I had been gone for the last two weeks, and Kevin was home alone; maybe it meant nothing and somehow the hair just got caught on a piece of clothing and coincidently just dropped on the floor.

September 1995

Later that same week, in September 1995, while Kevin was at school, the phone rang; this was before cell phones were a thing, and I answered the phone in the kitchen.

"Hello?" I asked.

"Is Kevin there?" asked a female voice on the phone.

"No, I'm sorry he's not."

"Oh, okay, I'll call him later then," she replied hesitantly.

"Can I give him a message and tell him who's calling?" I asked.

"Um, well, yes, can you tell him that Heather called, and I can't meet him at the gym tomorrow. Um, we're supposed to work on a project together for, um, a work project." She stammered awkwardly.

I was puzzled. I paused and then replied, "Okay, I'll give him the message."

After she hung up, I thought, *What on earth was that all about? Who is Heather, and what's this job meeting at the gym? Why is Kevin having plans to meet with a woman at the gym?* I was so uncomfortable after speaking with this strange woman on the phone.

I knew Kevin worked out at the campus gym, and he put a workout area together in our basement so I could exercise at home while looking after the children. He meets with a woman at the gym, while he lets me work out at home in the basement. *How conveniently generous of him,* I thought. I was upset and confused.

I went to Kevin's study and looked at the picture he kept of his work crew. There were a handful of men and a couple of women, and their names were listed on the picture. My finger followed the picture until I came to a "Heather." She was very pretty and had long, brown hair. Was she the reason there was a long, brown hair on my bathroom floor? Was this woman in my house with Kevin while I was away with the girls? My mind was spinning with unanswered questions that only Kevin could answer. I checked his course schedule and noticed he had two hours of free time around his lunch break the next day. I pondered how I would confront Kevin about this situation.

The day was long; the kitchen was finally clean, the kids were bathed, and it was finally time for us to go to bed. I was exhausted and spent, and I was nervous as I felt my heart pump with anxiety in my chest. As I got ready for bed, I casually conversed with Kevin.

"Hey, I was hoping to get out of the house with the girls tomorrow and thought that we could meet you on campus for lunch?"

"Ah, well, actually, tomorrow won't work," he responded with hesitancy. "I won't have enough time."

"But I saw you had two hours off for a lunch break tomorrow. We won't take much of your time. I'd love to see you, and the kids would be ecstatic to see Daddy for lunch. I'd also like to swing by the pool and check out the children's swim lessons. I think the girls should get swim lessons."

I wanted to hear his side of the situation before I jumped to any conclusions about his hidden meeting and relationship with Heather.

As we both got into bed, he continued, "Well, I have to study over lunch, so don't bother going to the pool. I can check out the swim schedule for you."

"That's okay," I replied. "I look forward to getting the kids out for a bit, and I can look into the pool schedule with the girls by myself, if you don't have time to fit us into your schedule."

I was quietly upset by now as he continued to insist that I not come by with the girls to the campus pool. The pool was right across from the gym. Kevin knew I would see him with another woman.

He grew uncomfortably insistent as he had his back turned to me in bed and said, "Don't bother. I will check it out for you."

I paused the conversation and said, with a question, "Oh?" and then continued, "Oh, by the way, Heather called today and said she can't meet you at the gym tomorrow."

He paused long, and with his back still turned to me, he took a deep breath in and then said, "Oh, yeah? Thank you for reminding me. I was supposed to meet her at the gym to discuss some work project."

What on earth? I thought to myself and reached to turn out the bedside light. How could he just cover up his secret meeting with another girl with another blatant lie? I was upset and had a difficult time getting to sleep that night. There were no work projects that took place at a gym.

I prayed and quietly held back silent tears.

My discoveries shook the reality of my truth, and I questioned the picture of what I thought an ideal marriage was. It's not supposed to be this way. A wife shouldn't have to discover and stumble upon evidence of secret relationships. She shouldn't have to intercept questionable phone calls and find evidence of pornography, questionable cards, and love notes. Husbands are not supposed to have secret relationships and meet other women for dates. That's supposed to stop when you're married, right?

A marriage should be based on truth and honor, yet my quest for the truth is met with another lame denial and sheepish excuse that tries to cover up reality with another lie.

I was so distraught and disturbed since the evidence was blatantly obvious. He was lying. He was alone at home by himself for the last two weeks when I was gone away with the girls, and now, I'm dealing with lies and evidence of him having secret meetings with another woman.

The sun went down, and the moon placed a shadow across our blanket, covering the unanswered questions of that day. My heart pounded with anger from the betrayal and lies I had discovered that day. The deceit was so evident. I quietly held back silent tears as I prayed.

Then, I fell asleep.

> In your anger do not sin. Do not let the
> sun go down while you are still angry, and
> do not give the devil a foothold.
> —Ephesians 4:26–27

Early Autumn 1995

The last part of summer disappeared as the autumn leaves started to change color from green to orange and yellow. The sun laced through the golden hues of the rustling leaves, giving way to the brilliant blue sky above. The fresh yet warm breeze of September made my senses tingle with anticipation. I loved this time of year, and I loved being out with the kids. I couldn't wait to surprise him. It was a perfect day, and since I was doing errands with the girls close to Kevin's work, I thought we'd stop to say hi to Daddy. His work position was quite casual and didn't demand performance until he was called on active duty.

The girls were squealing with delight and hurrying out of the van, excited to see where Daddy worked. I propped baby Everleigh on my hip, held Brooklyn's little hand, and walked across the parking lot as Makenna skipped alongside us. It was rare that Kevin was out on duty, so I was certain he'd be happy to see me and the girls.

The girls and I went into the foyer of the building, and a young woman greeted us and asked if she could help me.I told her I was Kevin's wife and I was here to see him.

She looked surprised, furrowed her eyebrows, and asked, "Kevin's married, and he has kids?"

"Yes," I replied with annoyance that she should even question me about Kevin being married with children. Shouldn't she know this if she worked with Kevin so often? Then I saw her name badge and realized it was Heather, the young woman on the phone call I intercepted, the one who was planning to meet Kevin at the gym. I felt sick to my stomach, and I was annoyed and uncomfortable with how she addressed me.

My mind was a blur, and my thoughts were distracted after that introduction. I thought to myself, *It didn't make sense. Why would he keep me, his wife, and his little girls a secret from those he worked with?*

As I waited on the couch with the girls to see Kevin, Heather commented, "I didn't know Kevin was married with children. He's such a nice guy, and he's such a good hugger."

My mind shouted inside my head as I thought to myself, *Did I just hear that right? Seriously, did she just say Kevin was such a good hugger? She did! What was my husband doing hugging this co-worker?*

I sank into the couch, recounting her words that echoed in my mind. I stopped in silence as my eyes fixated on the nothingness of the floor. I felt like I was a no one to him. His three daughters and I should've come up in conversation at some point.

Then I thought about how he didn't wear his wedding ring anymore; he said it was a hazard to wear at work.

No biggie, right? I thought, trying to console my suspicious mind and calm my racing heart. I don't remember if I left or stayed there with the girls. My thoughts collided with my jealousy and halted in a storm cloud of disappointment and suspicion. I did not like how this meeting made my heart sink.

I felt like the girls and I meant nothing to him. This feeling met me right in that hidden dark closet of despair, the place in my soul where I felt alone, with the door shut, unaware of the world in that moment. I felt betrayed. I hugged my three girls to sidetrack me from my new and questionable reality. I decided to shake the experience, and the suspicion, out of my mind. I was sure my imagination was making something bigger out of this than I should allow, right?

> The heart is deceitful above all things and beyond cure. Who can understand it?
> —Jeremiah 17:9

Dear Younger Me:

Do you not see that the Holy Spirit speaks to you in your dreams and through metaphors and types? He forewarns you of overwhelming and possibly deceptive times ahead. The dream is of a ringmaster, like the one who directs your life and your marriage. If you pray and stay in the center of the master's ring, the center of God's will in your marriage, then you will be protected through the fearful attacks and trials that come your way.

Life and marriage will throw all kinds of spiritual attacks and temptations in your direction, but dear Younger Me, there's a protective place in Jesus. Remain in the center of God's will and our Master's provision of safety, but don't disregard your intuition and the red flags you encounter along the way.

Whoever dwells in the shelter of the Most High will rest in the shadow of the Almighty.

I will say of the Lord, "He is my refuge and my fortress, my God, in whom I trust."

Surely, he will save you from the fowler's snare and from the deadly pestilence.

He will cover you with his feathers, and under his wings you will find refuge;

his faithfulness will be your shield and rampart.

You will not fear the terror of night, nor the arrow that flies by day.

—Psalm 91:1–5

But I tell you that anyone who looks at a woman lustfully has already committed adultery with her in his heart.

—Matthew 5:28

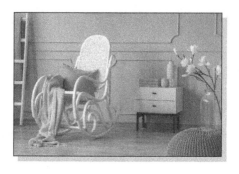

Chapter 14

THE VIEW FROM MY ROCKING CHAIR

December 1995

Life skipped right into a busy Christmas holiday time, and the vacation I took with the girls to California, for my cousin's wedding, was now just a memory as we embarked on moving to a new home. Each room now had boxes full of memories containing all the items that represented us and our fun experiences as a family.

I can't believe how much we've accumulated over the years, I thought to myself. Even though I looked forward to moving from our newer home into a more affordable and older house, I still wondered how we had accumulated so much stuff. Will we need all this stuff, and should I get rid of it or pack it up in a box? It seemed like a bittersweet task as I sorted through all the girls' clothes and toys and our family's belongings.

As I rocked myself on the white rocking chair and viewed everything in Everleigh's nursery, I thought about all I loved here, these people, this house, and everything in this room. *I love this rocker that I sanded and painted from brown to white and rocked and nursed my babies in.* I found some lovely matching fabric that coordinated with the Laura Ashley printed curtains I sewed for the baby room. The padded seat cover was just another way I expressed being creative and saved money with DIY projects.

There's so much poverty and wars going on in the world, and anyone could attest to that fact when you turn on the news. I thank God for all His blessings and protection right now. *I have so much*, I thought as I looked around at the stacked boxes of all our precious stuff.

Kevin has gone back to school again to get another degree, and although his workload is extremely taxing, he is enjoying it very much. The doors of engineering have closed for him, and the new pursuit to get another degree should open many new windows of opportunity. He's been a hard-working provider, waking up early to go to school or work, then coming back home to eat, sleep, and study, before he goes back to work again. We cannot wait for his university schooling to be done. Even though Kevin's rarely home, we still manage to steal away our private moments, and having three babies in four years is proof of our intimate love.

The doctor told me I couldn't have babies when we were first married, but thank God, like a miracle, we had three beautiful daughters that were obviously meant to be. Our children were a gift from God. Apart from a few heart-sinking blips in our marriage, we shared a very loving and satisfying life together. God has blessed us, and we have much to be thankful for. I only wish we had more time to have fun together, and go out, and do some of the things we used to do before we had children and before his university pursuits.

I've enjoyed fulfilling educational pursuits through correspondence courses. I'm not sure if I will get the chance to work any time soon, but it gives me a sense of accomplishment to get some diplomas. If you were to look into my soul, aside from my main passion in my marriage and my family, you would find a passion for flowers and the deep desire to master the art of language in written form. There seems to be very little time for that now, but I did promise myself I would finish a book by the time I turned eighty.

I feel a sense of contentment in this moment right now as I rock myself in this rocking chair of peace. These moments of quiet are few and far between; they don't seem to happen enough with the three kids and a husband in school. The house is silent except for the tick of the clock and the hum of the fluorescent light bulbs. I breathe in the fragrance of eucalyptus that lingers in the air from the candles Kevin bought me for Christmas. The laundry is freshly folded, the house is clean, the kids are bathed and sleeping, and the filled moving boxes are stacked in the corners of the rooms. I am exhausted, yet everything is in its place, and I pause to remember the good times we shared as a family, together in this home.

When I get to heaven, I would love to ask God why children are such a dear treasure and blessing in our lives, yet why do they take the stuffing right out of us and cause us to feel absolutely drained?

Makenna is such a sweet mamma love and eager to please these days. She loves to color, and now that she's almost five and in kindergarten, she is copying many words and wanting to spell. She can do pretty much anything she puts her mind to. She presses her lips together, squints her eyes, and although she is so slight, she manages to make the biggest and cutest chipmunk cheeks. She told us the other day that she likes it when we kiss, although she tries to nuzzle her way in between us.

Brooklyn, our little gem, is always the first to join us in the morning, looking for a quiet, warm hug. I love the way she kicks her leg back to make a funny type of baby bunny, hop circle, while making a growly squeal with her voice. She makes us laugh with love to the moon and back. If I were to capture anything right now for you, Brooki, my sweet daughter, it would be the way you snuggle up for a close-to-my-heart hug while I sing you lullaby bed-time songs of "Kindlein Mein," "Schlaff, Schlaff," and "Somewhere Over the Rainbow." You have the softest touch and love to stroke my cheek.

Tonight, as I kissed my three little girls and tucked them in for the night, Makenna said, "Mommy, merry Christmas," and Brooklyn said, "Yes, Mommy, and a shiny new mirror too."

The things children come up with are so funny. A "happy New Year," in her ears, was "a shiny new mirror." How darling is that? Brooklyn, or as we call her, Brooki, is our coloring queen and loves rubbing chalk all over the chalkboard. The same piece of art will be three different things.

"Look, Mommy, it's a waterfall," or, "Look, Mommy, it's a snowstorm," or, "Look, Mommy, it's fog."

You just can't make up these things. These precious sayings and sometimes words of truth really do come from the mouth of babes.

Everleigh, now being two weeks away from two years old, is talking up a storm. She says, "I love you, Mommy and Daddy," straight out of the blue. They say that "out of the blue" is a message from heaven. I believe our precious children are in direct communication with the angels before they can speak.

Our children bring messages from the Holy Spirit and from heaven, if we just stop to listen. Just a couple of weeks ago, Everleigh's message of, "I love you," sounded like, "Red shoes." She still loves her bottle and her blanket, which she calls gigi, and she doesn't want to give in totally to going potty. Today, it was one successful potty dance out of six. I love how she giggles so robustly when Daddy chases her around the house. If I was to freeze-frame a moment with Everleigh, it would be last night when I went to gaze upon her angelic form as she slept soundly in her crib. Her soft, white-blonde, shoulder-length hair swept across her forehead, and her perfect features were enough to melt my heart.

I sighed and said, "Oh, sweet daughter of mine, aren't you precious and peaceful as you are sleeping and dreaming with the angels?"

What a relief to know the babies are asleep and clean, fed, and safe in their beds. This is but a brief moment of relief when Everleigh is sleeping, for when she's awake, she's a never-ending, ongoing concern.

A wonderful, handsome, and hard-working husband, three beautiful, healthy daughters, and a lovely home; what more could a girl ask for?

> I consider that our present sufferings are not worth comparing with the glory that will be revealed in us.
>
> —Romans 8:18

> And we know that in all things God works for the good of those who love him, who have been called according to his purpose.
>
> —Romans 8:28

Chapter 15

A FEW REALLY
BAD AND GOOD-FOR-
NOTHING DAYS

October 1995

It was a very lovely warm day in early October when I decided to take Brooklyn and Everleigh for a stroller walk to pick Makenna up from kindergarten. It was an unseasonably warm day, and I was determined to enjoy the weather while we still could before the snow changed into freezing slush and muddy puddles. It wasn't a long walk, maybe twenty minutes or so, and it was a perfect day to stop and play at the park between Makenna's school and our home. The two little ones squealed with excitement and agreed that it was a very good idea to go to the park.

Off we went, Brooklyn at least five feet ahead, running in her excited long sprint as she always did, and me behind, pushing the stroller with Everleigh inside, enjoying the ride. Once we picked up Makenna, we continued with our plan to stop at the park, to play on the slide, and to swing on the swings. It was a perfect day to enjoy the warm sun on our faces and the glowing colors of the golden fall leaves fluttering to the ground. These warm days of autumn were few and far between. It felt so good to enjoy maybe one of the last runs on the green grass before fall turned into the frosty chill of the winter.

We hadn't expected the change in the weather. I didn't see the big, gray cloud until it started blocking the sunshine. I thought it was going to be an uninterrupted day with clear blue skies, but the clouds appeared. The gray clouds turned ominous. I gathered the girls and said we needed to head back home.

Of course, the girls weren't too happy to leave that fun park and time of play. They weren't watching the sky or the clouds, and quite frankly, the change in weather came so quickly that it caught me off guard as well. The cloud cracked with thunder, and then a bolt of lightning sent us dashing from the park and up to the sidewalk, as the floodgates of heaven opened in a fury and sunshine changed to pelting rain.

The rain came down fast and furiously as I zipped up the girls' warm raincoats. Thank goodness they had hats attached to their coats, and thank goodness for the stroller awning over baby Everleigh. We hurried up to the safety of home, and I thought we could make it home if we just hurried. Then it happened: The wheel on the stroller fell off.

"What? Are you kidding me?" I shouted. "How could this very good day turn into such a very, very bad day?"

The girls and I were in full panic mode; the weather had turned from full sunshine into torrential rain in sixty seconds or less. We were soaked. My three little girls were crying. We couldn't decipher our tears from the pelting raindrops that dripped down our faces and soaked our coats. Those twenty minutes, dragging a broken stroller with a baby on my hip, and with my other two little girls begging to be carried and protected from the rain, were some of the longest and most difficult moments I spent as a mom. All a mother wants to do is to protect her little ones from the harsh weather and rainstorms of life.

We finally got home after the longest twenty minutes of our rainy and stormy day; we toweled ourselves off and exchanged our cold and wet clothes for a warm blanket and comfy couch. What a relief to be home in our dry and safe home, where we could have a hot cup of cocoa and curl up on the couch to read a good book and plan what kind of theme cake we were going to make for Makenna's fifth birthday. We were dry, we were warm, and our world was all right again, at least for this moment after that rainstorm passed.

We decided on making a Pebbles Flintstone birthday cake, and I was copying the image of the Pebbles napkins I bought from the party store onto the white icing I spread all over the chocolate cake I made that morning. My mom taught me that as long as I had family gathered, and I made a cake with some icing, candles, a hat, and a few presents, you had a birthday party. We didn't have a big party to celebrate Makenna's mid-week fifth birthday, but I made a big deal out of it for our little family.

We ate a special supper, and I had the cake, specially iced in bright colors. McKenna had her birthday hat on, and the candles were ready to be lit. The girls' eyes were eager with anticipation to sing the happy birthday song, and the only one missing from this party was Daddy. Kevin was still downstairs, so I called him to come up so we could light the five candles on the cake to celebrate Makenna's birthday.

Twenty minutes passed; it was getting late. It was like a lifetime for three little girls waiting for birthday candles to be lit and wanting to eat cake. The girls needed to get to bed since it was already 7:00 p.m., and I still had to bathe them before bed. The girls were anxious and waiting, and I was tired and frustrated after cleaning the supper dishes and trying to put this little party together by myself. I tried to make it a special memory for Makenna and her sisters. Would they remember this day? Would they know how hard I tried to make it special, even though it seemed simple? I made the effort. I tried, but where was Kevin? Why was he making us wait so long? Did he even care that it's his daughter's birthday?

I was disappointed that he was making us wait; the girls had to go to bed, and it was getting late. I went downstairs to ask him to come upstairs so we could light the birthday candles and sing "Happy Birthday."

His study door was locked. Why was his study door locked? Why wasn't he answering me? I was upset and wondered what he could be doing behind the locked door. Why did he keep putting us off?

I knocked loudly on his door again and said, "Aren't you coming upstairs to help celebrate Makenna's birthday? It's getting late, and the girls and I are waiting for you so we can light candles and eat cake. What's taking you so long? Why is your door locked?"

When I knocked again, the door burst open.

To my surprise, Kevin grabbed me around my throat by my shirt collar. My excitement of celebration was exchanged for shock and fear. He picked me up with his strong arm and slammed me into the stairs.

My back ribs hurt. I was stunned and gasping for breath. I quietly sobbed on those cold, hard stairs.

I tried to pull myself together, but I don't really remember the rest of that evening too well, except for the picture I snapped of Makenna and the girls wearing birthday hats, ready to blow out the candles on the cake in front of them.

The picture of the birthday celebration was a reminder of their joy, yet it was a reminder of the fear, the pain, and silent disappointment I tried to forget. The girls would never know about that very bad and painful moment. I never talked about it. I wanted them to remember the fun birthday party and that day at the park, before the rainstorm came.

Maybe I shouldn't have knocked on the door so harshly; maybe he wouldn't have been so mad, and maybe he wouldn't have hurt me the way he did if I didn't insist on him joining us for birthday cake. I don't know, but it was hard to breathe. I wanted to forget the twenty minutes just before we lit the celebration candles. I suppressed it and locked it away, so as not to remember.

Later, Kevin said he was very sorry and regretted hurting me, and now thinking back to that memory, I see I was very flippant about what happened because I knew I was hurt. I could move on and forgive, so I swept the memory under the carpet, yet I was still broken.

> I have told you these things, so that in me you may have peace. In this world you will have trouble. But take heart! I have overcome the world.
>
> —John 16:33

> The Lord is a refuge for the oppressed, A stronghold in times of trouble.
>
> —Psalm 9:9

Chapter 16

FALL FROM GRACE

May 2022

My eyes stung from tears mixed with eye cream, smudged mascara, and the strain of reading the years of journals strewn across the mattress on the floor of this tiny new condo I now call home.

I came to the middle of *A Mother's Journal: A Keepsake Book for Thoughts and Dreams* and considered the next pages. The pages were blank and whispered a loud silence. Somewhere between the winter of 1995 and the spring of 1997, the pages were white. My words stopped and went without rest on the paper. My pen ran out of ink, for over two years. Where did my fairytale story stop? What were those words that remained unspoken and hidden in my dark closet of time, those words that were too painful to be set in ink and too painful and shameful to find rest on the white pages of my journals. I imagine a big "X" over the words that could've been written, but instead, there was nothing. Nothing but a clean, blank slate of pages to consider the cutting truth.

Winter 1996

The associate pastor walked down from the pulpit with his eyes focused on each step away from his humiliating confession that Sunday evening. The congregation shuffled uncomfortably in their seats as if they were all sitting naked on a scratchy, woolen pew. They all froze in hushed and stunned perplexity at how a pastor could stray so far away from his calling and how he could betray his wife of twenty-something years. What were his teenage children thinking as their father gave that revealing and cutting confession?

"Does anyone else have anything to add or say before the members vote to accept the resignation of the associate pastor?" the senior pastor asked the congregation.

Who would dare add anything to this hushed silence? The atmosphere seemed weighty and thick, and the congregation looked as though they were holding their breath through choking ash after a raging fire. It felt as though a double-edged sword sliced down and back through the heaviness of the air and silenced its prey in one fell swoop.

Everyone from the age of sixteen to one hundred and six showed up for the evening service that night. The senior pastor announced earlier that day, in the morning service, that there was going to be a meeting at tonight's evening service. The meeting would be an adult-only topic, with a sensitive undertone, and members should keep their younger children at home.

"Is there anyone else who wants to come up to say something?" the senior pastor repeated as the disappointed assistant pastor took his seat beside his wife and family.

Then she stood up. She was the other woman. Her numb feelings made her feel out of body as if she was walking beside herself. Her husband walked beside her down the aisle. They were broken, as husband and wife, as they walked down the church aisle together, to the front of the pulpit. They turned to face the congregation and stopped in front of the large, wooden pulpit, thankful to be half-hidden with something to lean on. They paused and heard a shriek of anguish from an older lady in the congregation.

"No," she shouted in disbelief.

Her eye met with the older lady's disappointed gaze. She recognized the older lady as her mom's dear friend. The older lady, who shrieked out loud, had known the lovely young lady since she was a baby. She was the young mom with the sweet singing voice in the choir; she was the one who taught Sunday school, and now she was the one, standing in front of the pulpit, as the guilty look before confession. The older lady felt sick, and she didn't want to hear it. She didn't want to know why her younger friend was ready to speak into the microphone that Sunday evening.

All eyes stayed glued to the younger couple as they reluctantly spoke in front of the entire congregation. The young wife and mom proceeded in a broken voice. She took a deep breath to try to calm her fear and blinked hard to clear the tears.

She could not sit by and watch the pastor take the

entire blame of the fall, for she was also not above reproach. The entire congregation needed to know the reason why he was resigning. The congregation only knew he was resigning because there was an indiscretion, and he was stepping down from his position of assistant pastor. He taught and cared for the youth in the church in a godly way, and that was his soul's desire: to teach about Christ's love.

She proceeded to speak into the microphone, in front of the entire congregation, and she needed the congregation to know their teen children were always cared for and taught in a godly manner. No indiscretion ever involved any of their children.

She proceeded with a broken voice and said, "I was also in youth ministry, and you trusted us with your teens, but we fell as adults, and we failed you as leaders and teachers in the church. I started a relationship that was not mine to have. We are both married, and our love and devotion should have been solely for our own spouses, and for that, I am truly sorry, and ask my God, my husband, and the other man's wife, family, and all of you to please forgive me for what I have done. I will also step down as an assistant in the youth ministry and from any ministry that I was part of in the church.

I failed you and I truly regret what I did … and I am so, so sorry … and again I ask for your forgiveness. Thank you for your grace, mercy, and prayers as we seek godly counsel and try to amend our broken relationship with our spouses."

She stood beside herself, and her husband stood by her. They then left the pulpit, walked down the aisle of the sanctuary, slipped out the back door, and left the church.

Their marriage was torn asunder, and she held back tears as they drove back home in silence. She pressed her infamous speech, that she prepared on a single-ruled piece of paper, crinkled in her clutched hand. She stared out of the van window and wondered how this all came to be.

How had all of this transpired over just a couple months and a few misinterpreted meetings? How did working on a ministry project turn into, "I'm going to miss you"? How did I ever even say those words to him? How could I, as a Christian, who knew better, betray my own husband and the other man's wife like that? How did my wrong choices disappoint and betray so many? Could Jesus still forgive me? Jesus, forgive me, she thought as another tear fell down her cheek.

She felt like the woman at the well, and the unnamed woman caught in adultery, in the Bible in John 8. It felt like she was wearing an exit costume of a black cape with a red letter "A" sewn on the back of her cape.

How did one lunch date, a couple of letters from the heart, and a couple planned meetings turn into this? She thought about the time she spent together with the pastor. Even though she'd been a Christian since she was a child, she now felt shamelessly careless in her Christian walk.

She had so many questions when she worked alongside the assistant pastor. She was happy to have an eager ear to listen and ask each other questions about their faith. She kept her real painful memories hidden from him, and she was happy to have someone talk to her and seem to care for her in her busy days of motherhood and lonely days of being married to a husband who was rarely home. She felt someone cared and wanted to really know her and her depths of being.

She knew what she was doing was wrong, and she thought about how they talked about the difference between just thinking about flirting with boundaries and crossing boundaries. What did it matter since God saw both of those crossed boundaries as being the same?

They discussed how all they had to do was look at each other in the wrong way, and God would consider that as a sin as well.

They justified their secret meetings, all in the name of helping each other find answers to their apparent midlife crisis. Yet, they didn't consider the fallout their loved ones would experience because of their poor choices and betrayal. They really didn't know each other; they were just caught up in the exhilarating feeling of the moment to be truly known, and they knew they did love their own spouses. She wondered at what point in their relationship they crossed the line.

None of it mattered anymore. All she wanted to do was be forgiven and cared for. She didn't realize that underneath her actions, she just wanted her husband to feel the same pain that his betrayal brought her the year previous. She wanted her husband to care for her and love her, but she never imagined how this wrong choice could crush their spirits so deeply.

She was eternally grateful for forgiveness and grace, and she was so thankful that it was over, and the shame of it being out in the open and public was a great burden to carry. It was too heavy, but for the grace of Jesus, her Savior.

She was an honest person and couldn't live a lie, and she knew that when her husband started to ask questions like, "Why were you talking on the phone so long with him? Are you having an affair?" she had to confess and admit, even to herself, that, maybe when defining the word, whether emotional, or physical, that was the truth of the matter. When confronted, she had to be honest and vulnerable to tell him the whole, regretful truth.

She had to say, "Yes, I guess, that was what it was."

Thank God she still had a husband who stood by her side. She reached over to put her hand on his hand as he drove the car home. They gave each other the knowing look of, *I still love you*, and the long blink of, *We'll get through this*, and *I'll still always be by your side*.

Over the next couple of months, they shared moments of grievous tears and hugged each other like their survival depended on it. As a broken husband and wife, they listened to music and worship songs together flat out on the ground. He started to write her inspiring and romantic letters, and his words made her feel beautiful again. They went to four counselling sessions; two alone and two together, that revealed their different and unique personality types, and they were given books to read.

They talked more and even shared romantic bubble

baths together, and their passionate physical expressions of love brought their relationship to a new frontier of expressing their feelings within. The duty of work and family life was still there, but now they didn't take anything for granted, and they made time for exciting date nights together. They were committed to making their relationship work.

She answered his every question and disclosed every step she took, that car ride alone to the grocery store, and every phone call. She had to rebuild the walls of broken trust. They were two broken pieces that were torn asunder, yet they were on the path to a new start together as husband and wife.

She embraced Jesus's powerful forgiveness and mercy, and she was overwhelmed and so thankful that her husband extended his forgiveness to her. She never wanted to be labeled with the scarlet letter A. She wanted a new name and wasn't proud of her old name anymore. But somehow, through God's grace, she slowly moved past her shame and gratefully stepped back into her role of being a loving wife and a mom. She was eternally grateful for another chance.

They were healing together as a couple and extremely happy to close that chapter of their life.

There was a new chapter in their life filled with new commitments, family vacations, birthday celebrations, poetry, and slow dances to the songs in the living room.

> For all have sinned and fall short of the glory of God, and all are justified freely by his grace through the redemption that came by Christ Jesus.
>
> —Romans 3:23–24

Have mercy on me, O God, according to your unfailing love; according to your great compassion blot out my transgressions. Wash away all my iniquity and cleanse me from my sin.

Cleanse me with hyssop, and I will be clean; wash me, and I will be whiter than snow.

Hide your face from my sins and blot out all my iniquity.

Create in me a pure heart, O God, and renew a steadfast spirit within me.

Do not cast me from your presence or take your Holy Spirit from me.

Restore to me the joy of your salvation
and grant me a willing spirit, to sustain me.

—selected verses from Psalm 51

Slow Dance
David L. Weatherford

Have you ever watched kids on a merry-go-round,
or listened to the rain slapping on the ground?
Ever followed a butterfly's erratic flight
or gazed at the sun into the fading night?

You better slow down, don't dance so fast
Time is short and the music won't last.

Do you run through each day on
the fly? When you ask,
"How are you?" Do you hear the reply?
When the day is done, do you lie in your bed
With the next hundred chores
running through your head?

You'd better slow down, don't dance so fast
Time is short and the music won't last.

Ever told your child, we'll do it tomorrow
And in haste, not see his sorrow?
Ever lost touch, let a good friendship die
Cause you never had time to call and say, "Hi?"

You'd better slow down don't dance so fast
Time is short and the music won't last.

When you run so fast to get somewhere
You miss half the fun of getting there
When you worry and hurry through your day
It is like an unopened gift …
Thrown away …
Life is not a race. Do take it slower
Hear the music, Before the song is over.

Chapter 17

NEW BEGINNINGS: JANUARY 1, 1998

It's been two years since we moved from Alberta to BC; we started a brand-new beginning back in our hometown, where our extended family lived. We built a new home for ourselves, and we experienced much mercy and blessings these past years.

Now, on this New Year's Day, I begin to feel contractions; I'm sure this will be the day we have our fourth baby. Even though the contractions have been regular, their nonproductivity in the delivery department only prove how God is always in control. He has His set time for everything.

On another snowy day in January 1998, our fourth blessing, Ellie Faith, came to us, wrapped in a pink blanket. Her first newborn outfit was a waffle knit, cotton, lumberjack-type of sleeper and a baby blue hat with mittens to match, in the slim chance that she might be a boy. Pink or blue, it didn't matter, and I guess we were meant to have a team of girls. God has a miraculous way of pouring out blessings when we continue in love and make a choice to stay close and committed to our loved ones.

Christmas once again passed by so very quickly; it was one of our busier Christmases in comparison to others. It was common for us to go from one home to the other, visiting two sets of grandparents, multiple sisters and brothers, aunts, and uncles. It was such a welcome change to spend the actual Christmas Eve and Christmas morning by ourselves, as our own little family. We needed those quiet days, away from the hustle and bustle of extended family. This year, the song went like this: "Two turkey dinners and one hectic and a messy Christmastime."

It's amazing all that can happen in two years. Part

of me never wants to forget the memories of that time, and another part of me wants to always remember how we came through the tests and trials with God by our side. We are in a new place here in our relationship. Kevin and I have come through these last years of selfish pursuit, loneliness, stubbornness, deceit, turmoil, heartache, tears, and shame, yet, somehow, by the grace of God, we still ended up with blessings, triumph, and unspeakable joy. Can I look back and consider the trials we came through as joy? I think so, and I know this man I married is the man of my dreams, and I am totally devoted to this thing we call love and marriage.

Since moving back closer to where our family lived, Kevin is now working for his dad at Livingston Corp. He's also been the general contractor on our new house that we excitedly moved into just before Christmas. It goes without saying that with our fourth new baby, building a new home, and starting a new career, we are very busy.

I wonder when life will slow down. Picking out interior décor between being taxi mom has been a bit hectic, but I'm sure every mom goes through similar experiences. One day, I might find the time to finish the bookkeeping course I started, and finish sewing my curtains, but until then, I'm sure I will always say I have too much to do.

This year will once again find me knee-deep in diapers and laundry, but I am looking forward to life with baby Ellie completing our family. I couldn't imagine what my life would look like without the four beautiful daughters God blessed us with.

This last year was a year of rediscovering what it meant to be a mom of a newborn and three other busy little girls. I also squeezed in some time to enjoy a few of my own creative passions, like singing, piano, painting, and writing. God willing, I will grow and age alongside Kevin, and we can both discover many of our cherished dreams along the way. Until then, I pray that God allows me to see each step I take in a new light. This light that focuses on my husband, and children, and their splendor within these walls we call home will satisfy me and encourage my heart.

I long to always remember my children's hugs, laughter, creativity, and innocence, and even how their hair smells after a bath. I want to remember how their tiny fingers feel in mine and how they danced with their daddy. There are so many wonderful things I want etched into our memories, and times of being burnt-out, cranky parents are not any I want to remember. The girls are my little gems. Sometimes they need a bit of polishing, but they are, after all, just little children, and the learning process can be challenging at times.

Makenna is now seven and in grade two. She's a bright little thing, who loves friends and wants to be included. Artwork seems to be her passion as well as playing learning games on the computer. Makenna can get discouraged sometimes and needs her self-esteem boosted, but that seems to be how we all are at times.

Brooklyn is now in kindergarten and five years old. She loves school and has great reasoning and common sense. She's quite fragile and tiny, which I attribute to her need to always be running instead of walking. It's so cute to watch her at the park. She runs everywhere; the other kids can't figure out if she's running away from them or chasing after them. Brooki wants to do so well at everything, and she can get her feelings hurt if something isn't perfect. She loves affection and is not afraid to show it. What a little charmer this gemstone is.

Wow, there's no stopping Everleigh. She is a spark waiting to light on fire. If Everleigh's energy is directed in the right way, she will be able to do great things. She's almost four and shows great signs of being very artistic and bright. She loves coloring, she's starting to write letters, and she loves talking. She sure knows how to express herself. She has great passion in tears and laughter, and loves to give compliments and show affection.

May 1998

"Mommy, did you know that I can snap my fingers?" Snap, snap, snap went Everleigh's fingers.

I looked quite amazed at what our little girl could do at the age of four. I said, "Yes, good girl," but did I really know? No, I don't think I did. I knew the laundry was piling up, and I knew the house became an organized disaster after morning rush hour, but I think I all too often overlooked the memory makers, even as simple as noticing a child learning how to snap her fingers.

I gaze out the window of our new baby nursery at our new home on the mountain. Now, here's a memory maker: I'm in my spring robe, a little smaller than it was a year ago; the sun is shining in the room while I'm surrounded by teddy bears and rocking horse wallpaper. Yet, nothing is more precious and memorable than our new baby, Ellie, staring up at me with her twinkling eyes. She was our 1 percent out of one hundred. Oh, how precious are these little ones who are gifted to us from our heavenly Father up above.

What is she thinking right now? I wonder as she watches the tears of joy well up in my eyes. As she falls asleep in my arms, I wonder if her forever unrecalled thoughts are those of our ancestors being replayed in her newborn dreams. One day we will know, but the mystery is ours to marvel at today.

I pause to whisper a prayer: "God, I thank You for our sweet Ellie. Thank You for this beautiful family You've given me."

These tears of joy stem from her perfection and the sweet sounds that come from her tiny soul. She has sweet character within her baby talk, as she makes sounds like "Ugee" and "Gula gula gula." I tuck her in her covers in her brown nursery crib, and I linger to watch as she sucks on her soother. I gaze at her delicate form as she lay asleep in her crib, which holds and protects her as she lay sleeping and unaware of the outside world.

I continued my prayer: "Oh God, protect our precious little ones from the evil and distaste of this world, and help us to bring them up in Your way, for they are made uniquely by You, in Your image. Forgive me for getting caught up in my everyday tasks that I fail to see Your miracle in these little ones You've given us to care for. Help me to be a mom and wife in honorable pursuit of Your character and leading. Lord, when I feel too exhausted and weary to keep up with the tasks of the day, please carry me and calm my fears. Please bless this new home and these precious lives within, and may we be pleasing and acceptable in Your sight. Amen."

I could write about our beautiful, new home, the home we built nestled in the pine trees, where snakes, cougars, and black widows come out to visit at night. I could write about our richness in family abundance or the beautiful mountains and weather here. I could even get into Kevin's business pursuits, but for now, and if only in the previous paragraphs and my continued prayer, let me invite you into my soul.

Here, with the prayer in my soul, words linger on one thought like the sun's shine on a leaf, unhindered by clouds. In my world of busyness, let me stop and wade in my pond of memories. Let my mind and heart ask me if the water is warm or if its iciness chills my bones. Here in my pond of peace, I wade in, covered by Jesus, supporting me from any currents caused by unwanted winds. I know that past these ponds in my imagined, quiet meadow is a place of hurry and interrupting sounds, yet I hold steadfast in this quiet moment of knowing all it takes is the throw of one small stone to cause a ripple and turbulence in my calm waters.

When the storm rages, Lord, I will reach for Your hands and look into Your eyes for strength and support. In any storm that may arise and cause waves to roll, Lord, I cling to You and look into Your eyes, for You are always with me. I'll walk out of the high waters and sit quietly in the cool grass, watching the warm sunshine peek through the clouds, and I'll feel the gentle breeze of Your Spirit kiss my cheeks.

Here in my calm and secret hiding place, I think to myself, *Why does the bird stay suspended in the air, or why would I worry about tomorrow if God looks after the sparrow?* One thing I know, as I sit alone here with my sleeping baby and in the presence of God, is that I should remember God's provision and His plan for our lives. He loves us so much. His creation is beautiful. This family and new baby of mine, and the birds that fly in the clear blue sky, are evidence of His glory. The

Lord protects me and blesses me, and I am left wanting nothing more.

May my words here in my journals be pleasing to You and somehow even bring You glory, Lord, Amen.

My older me continued to read the words in my journals written by my younger me. Now looking back at what I have written reminds me of the importance of taking account of this equity of love and trust, and recording our special moments in time. One day, life on this earth will no longer be ours but our children's time and then our grandchildren's time. What could be a more special gift for them than for a parent to write about their childhood, possibly one which they would otherwise never remember? I continue reading.

Makenna, you are our second little mommy at the age of seven. You've been a big help with your new baby sister. You are a bright girl who seems to always want to be older than you are. Maybe this is my fault for having put so many responsibilities on you. I love you, Makenna. You're my beautiful, little golden girl.

Brooklyn is like a springtime buttercup that dances in the breeze, tender and brilliant. I'll always remember your need to please and be loved. May no one ever step on your tender soul and springtime beauty.

Everleigh, you will go places. May God prepare your path so nothing will make you trip. You're my summer song dressed in a frilly laced slip with running shoes. I love your magnificent little life.

Ellie, you are our new direction, our special reminder of how life is supposed to be. You are gentle, yet full of life. You are confident, yet fragile, needing love and attention. I thank God for another opportunity to see His love through your complete smile and feel His tenderness in your tiny touch. Thank You, God, for Ellie. You're a sunbeam and a song on angel's wings, Ellie. Thank you for completing our family.

Our family is complete. Thanks to Kevin's love, strength, and continued commitment, we are complete. Yesterday was Mother's Day, a special day to celebrate the time we spend together. Kevin gave me the most beautiful watch. Right now, I look at it, and two things come to mind. One: I think I've wasted so much time writing today, but more importantly, two: I always want to spend my time with him. The watch is so pretty and feminine, yet creative, stylish, and sturdy, yet dainty with the perfect amount of genuine gold and silver. The description of the watch is what I can only hope he sees in me.

To my husband, my love,

We've walked through the fires of trial and crisis, and I want to thank you for your love, your forgiveness, and your grace. I also forgive you for the things you couldn't even talk about. I am overwhelmed with love that you would hold me like you'll never let me go. Thank you for your love letters to me.

To my sweet daughters,

I love you dearly to the moon and back. I pray that God will always keep your mom and dad close and in love and that you will know Jesus and that He will always keep you safe and secure in love. I wish you success in all your good pursuits and pray you will always keep family and faith in God dear to your heart. If we could erase all the mistakes of our past as though they never happened, and if we could go back and do it all over, we would. I would, and I'd do it better to prevent all the pains and heartache that come from poor choices. I can't change the past, but I can choose differently from now on, and I can only hope and pray that I will be a good parent and role model for you.

Consider it pure joy, my brothers and sisters, whenever you face trials of many kinds, because you know that the testing of your faith produces perseverance.

Let perseverance finish its work so that you may be mature and complete, not lacking anything.

—James 1:2–4

Chapter 18

THE JUNGLE DREAM: FEBRUARY 1999

Some of my dreams are so real, with character and color, and sometimes, they're so outrageous that I know I alone could not have come up with that clever metaphor or symbolic story. It's when these dreams stick so heavily on my mind that I ask why I had that dream. Is there a meaning or warning in the dream, and do certain characters in the dream represent someone or something?

My dream last night was about two carefree, rich, and entitled young safari travelers on a jungle hunt.

They didn't want to kill any animals per se, but they wanted to experience the hunt just for the sport of it. The girl had a potpourri posy of dried flowers around her neck to ward off bug bites, and the boy had a small canteen of water hanging from his neck. To me, these two safari travelers represented entitled young people, without regard, who just wanted to have fun and experience the best and the most in life. They didn't care about the cost or regard the destruction and chaos they created for anything else on their path. The posy around the girls' neck was a false hope and protection against the things of this world, and the boy's canteen of water was too meager for the journey.

To continue the story in my dream, here they were, two young travelers, on foot, wearing all the right safari clothes ready for the hunt, but they had no compass, no map, and no vehicle. The jungle was beautiful, covered in green moss, with the sun streaming through the trees and luscious ferns. In regardless haste, the two young travelers created a path of broken branches and cut down destruction of waste as they thrilled in the hunt. The atmosphere seemed to be beautiful, yet there was an adventurous sense of wilderness and danger lurking behind the jungle trees.

There was also a great lion roaring in the distance. The lion had a beautiful mane crowning his mighty head. In my dream and in my spirit-led understanding, to me, the lion represented the respected and majestic king of the jungle, like Aslan represented our Savior Jesus, in C.S. Lewis's novel, *The Lion, the Witch, and the Wardrobe.*

There were also two tall giraffes in my dream, who were comfortable in their habitat. To me, giraffes were tall and could see over and above and far over the land. Their lofty height and position is like some Christians with a holier than thou position, people who think they are better and above others, like rich people in a stately position. The high and mighty ones may not notice the lesser creatures below them or care about them. Their highness could become their weakness and cause them to stumble and bring about their great fall from grace. The Lord showed me that the giraffes represented arrogant Christians in leadership or leaders in high positions who take no notice of those below them; they think that grace sets them above the law.

The lion was leading the giraffes with its roar, yet the giraffes were too far off from the path to see the great lion or hear his roar. This great king of the jungle was there to protect and lead, but he was now too distant since the giraffes didn't stay near their protector and leader. This king of the jungle, the good leader, was all-knowing and had a keen sense of the dangers awaiting in the jungle.

The giraffes weren't always smart enough to follow and listen to the lion's roar, and at one time, they got too close to the careless humans who were out to have a good time. The two humans, the safari sport hunters, created chaos in the giraffe's environment and stirred up the peace. The two giraffes ran in different directions and tried to hide. The giraffes couldn't hear the lion's roar, their sense of direction and safety was confused, and they left destruction in their peaceful home and created a chaotic fury of mess behind.

Dear Younger Me,

These colorful dreams come to you at night as a gift that captures the message of the Holy Spirit's desire to awaken your soul to the missed messages and warnings in your day. Listen to the voice of the Holy Spirit. He wants to guide you through your journey, and he wants you to be wise and discerning with your husband, your family, friends, and leaders in the church.

Read the Bible, and stay close to God's leading and the quiet voice the Holy Spirit uses to speak to you as you navigate through this jungle journey called life. Be careful and considerate with your husband, but don't allow anyone or anything, like addictions, alcohol, lustful relationships, or pornography to come into your home. Talk to your spouse about the boundaries you need to set in place to have a blessed and honest marriage relationship. Be careful where you step, and don't become careless, or high and lofty with entitled arrogance. Stay close to God, pray to Jesus, and listen to His Spirit in you. God and His Word in the Bible will be your guide and your protection over your marriage and your children. Let God be the foundation upon which you build your marriage and family home.

August 1999

It's a brilliant August morning, with another hopeful day of sunshine and a high of 34 degrees Celsius beckoning us to seize the day. What a beautiful summer it's been. We've had many friends and family over and spent some fun days in my sister's swimming pool. The kids played soccer in the park and brought dripping popsicles into their cardboard playhouses they built in the pine trees just above our yard. I think the highlight of this summer was going to family camp. The girls took turns on the boat and jumped on the giant air blob that floated on the lake. We enjoyed listening to stories and prayed through the promises of God; we sang praises and roasted marshmallows by the campfire. What a great time to remember.

Whether my life is the reflection of my jungle dream, or whether I live in a zoo, I welcome the days of summer giving way to a more scheduled autumn. The days are getting cooler, yet these cozier days of fall and the beginning of the school year once again stir our desires to strive for accomplishments and get back to focused learning and regular bedtimes. These summer days, filled with the carefree and spontaneous moments of amusing kids, now slip away into a bittersweet time of getting back into early mornings and hectic routines.

I'm looking forward to enjoying some one-on-one time with Ellie between 10:00 a.m. and 2:00 p.m. I feel like the busy summer swept her away in the wake of her sisters and the crowd of neighborhood kids. There was a constant mound of dress-up clothes, sparkly and gluey crafts, and spaghetti sauce on the floor from the chaos of numerous lunchtime guests. I may even be able to steal away a few moments during Ellie's nap time to be selfish in my own studies and pursuits, or maybe I could even enjoy a nap or a bath in peace and quiet.

I strive for balance in our family schedules, the errands and shopping, laundry and ironing, taxi mom, baseball mom, Sunday school teacher, homework parent, teacher conferences, talent shows, piano lessons, suppertime, dishes time, bath time, story time, song time, and prayer time. And at the end of all that, I take my apron off, dust the flour off my face, and pull myself together.

I rub the glitter and glue off my fingers so I can still put on some blue high heels, curl up a sexy hairdo, and glide a pink lip gloss on my lips to remind my husband I may have a bit of energy left in me to even love him more and satisfy our desires while still being young and in love. I long to escape, to get away, and to dress up for date night with Kevin. Hey, a gal can still hope and dream, right?

At thirty-three years of age, I have a blessed and abundant life full of the hustle and bustle that a family of six brings with it, as well as the evidence of the stretch marks left on my tummy.

Their Unique, Young Selves

Makenna, being eight years old, is like a tweener going on twelve. She's a fun-loving little lady, finding balance between little girl, tomboy, and spicy clown. I can see beyond these young duckling years to her becoming like a beautiful swan. She tries to perfect everything she does, or maybe she wants to be perfect for her mommy and daddy and realizes that her curiosity can get the best of her, and she can lead her sisters astray. She tries to do the right thing in being a big sister, but sometimes, she's a bit secretive in her need for adventure. We may expect too much from our oldest daughter, and I fear that her posture can reflect her disappointment in not being perfect for us. We need to remind her and even ourselves to stand up tall and be proud of who God made us to be; it's okay not to be perfect.

Brooklyn, at seven years old, is still a petite little girl, like a waif of a fairy that belongs in the garden, free to run, jump, and fly around. My sweet daughter, you grow when the sun shines on you, and you thrive when you are watered with love. You are content with your alone time, yet you love to be loved and want to please everyone around you. There's no need to scold you, for your eyes get big with tears when you know you've done wrong. Your delicate soul reflects your outward, fawn-like beauty. You are helpful and kind, and everyone wants to be your friend.

Everleigh, you are a showstopper. Your laughter and expressive zest for life turn heads. You explode with the desire to express your creativity, your brilliant mind, and your desire to discover and learn. You have no fear. Just the other day, I heard you singing to yourself, "I think I can, I think I can, I know I can, I know I can," like the brave little choo-choo train trying to push up a steep mountain. You have the determination and strength of steel, yet a tender, loving, and fragile heart of glass. I pray that God directs your path, because once you get going, Everleigh, there's no stopping you. You're a tenacious, fun-loving, beautiful, and creative encourager. You are the third knock-out in the Livingston family.

Ellie, my sweetness, you are the reflection of beauties past and the hope of talent to come. At the age of one and a half, you are a tender-hearted caress and hug on

Sunday morning, and a feisty watch-where-you-step on Friday night. You are not made of many words yet, but you are made of every expression known to man and angels above. I think God wants you to stay speechless so the angels can talk and play with you a little longer. You don't speak yet, but you hum sweet, high-pitched songs where the heavenlies stop in awe, delight, and wonder in the beautiful creation of a little child. The rhythm and song are in your bloodstream, even when you sleep. You know when you've done something wrong, for you come back for a gentle hug. Your silky, sun-kissed blonde hair wisps away from your plump and rosy cheeks, giving way to your expressive little smile. That quirky little smile of yours is like sunshine being squeezed from a sweet and effervescent orange, and your bright blue-green eyes are like the sky's reflection in the tropical ocean. Your sweetness is alive and forgiving in every trouble to come.

March 2000

Upon the eve of another day, I thank God for the doors that are closing and a glimpse through the window of dreams to come. Kevin has just come back from a two-week work training course in the United States. His new career pursuits look hopeful and can help him in this new field of helping his father's family business grow.

> My sheep listen to my voice, I know them,
> and they follow me.
>
> —John 10:27

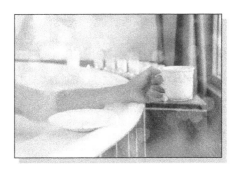

Chapter 19

HAPPY SATURDAY: JANUARY 2002

The snow came down like peaceful, fluffy white cotton last night. We woke to the sounds of snowblowers mimicking lawnmowers in the spring. Planes flew above while the vibration of the props echoed through the still cold, silence of the icy winter in January.

Makenna, Brooklyn, Everleigh, and Ellie started the busy buzzing sounds on this carefree and happy Saturday morning. Everleigh and Brooklyn greet Chancy, our golden boy dog, with a lively, "How ya doin', buddy?" Chancy grabbed an old stuffy toy with his mouth and gaily pranced toward any likely playmate to nuzzle an invitation for a tug-of-war.

Makenna looks outside at all the freshly fallen snow and sees dollar signs flashing before her eyes. Lately she's been an eleven-year-old with a passion for needing the new Nancy Drew book or Sims computer game. We're trying to teach the girls that all these wants and desires are like a bounty hunter coming with a price tag. Nevertheless, all the girls see the snow as an opportunity to shovel their way into the mall. Kevin and I see the snow as an opportunity to sneak past responsibilities of the day ahead.

We pulled our duvet cover back over our head and snuck a private kiss before discussing our dream of hopping a plane to Mexico and going scuba diving, something to allow us to escape this snowy and cold weather. Better judgment and a brief glimpse into our pocketbooks slammed the door shut on that dream, for now.

For now, I would have to embrace contentment in the thought of a leisurely bath, a casual eggs Benedict brunch that Kevin every so often spoiled us with, and a good morning latte. That was the way we were and how we'd say I love you as a family on a casual, happy Saturday morning.

"Knock, knock, knock," went a tap on our bedroom door. We heard that unmistakable, gentle thud on our door many times before.

Kevin and I give each other a knowing look and say, "Who is it?"

"It's me, Ellie."

Like we would never have known, we both think.

"What is it, Ellie?"

She just wants to go with her sisters to be part of the snow fun. Now that she's four, she can communicate so many needs and ideas to us. Lately, we find her playing with dolls and dressing up like a princess. She's a bubbly little girl with silky, soft, and long blonde hair, and her giggle is as genuine as the diamond set in my wedding ring.

After encouraging Ellie to find her snowsuit, Kevin puts on his new navy robe, and I take a leisurely bubble bath, welcoming a moment of quiet. I love and desire mornings like this, when Kevin brings a coffee to me in my bubble bath. It truly is a happy Saturday this morning. I love, and I am loved.

> Take delight in the Lord, and he will give
> you the desires of your heart.
> —Psalm 37:4

Chapter 20

BACK TO SCHOOL IN A NEW COUNTRY

January 2004

I munch on a rye bread sandwich as I reflect upon the memories past written by me, a mother and a wife who has taken once a year, maybe twice a year, to pen her thoughts of life's lessons and gifts of love through her family, her husband, and her children. Could it be that Makenna, the tiny baby I started writing about thirteen years ago in 1990, is the same girl who just made me this sandwich? I am blessed and ready for a new life in the United States. I am ready for the new opportunities that await us as we plan new pursuits.

It seems that just yesterday, I wrote about diapers and baby bottles, but the changes happen so quickly, and I find myself in a new place and time again. Who would have dreamed nine months ago that we would be living in a different country?

I remember a quiet time nine months ago, after I attended a Michael W. Smith worship concert at the Pepsi Stadium in Denver, Colorado. I asked the Lord for a new word, for the last words the Lord gave to sustain me over the last two years were *joy* and then *freedom*. Within an instant, the new word the Lord gave me set a new stage of things to come. The word he gave me was *change*. Boy, oh boy, did the Lord ever bring us into a new world of change.

I find myself looking out the window here in our rented home in Washington State and consider that we knew nobody except our friendly new neighbors. The government calls us "resident aliens," and that is precisely how we feel in this new environment, but we embrace the change with the excitement of living in the great US of A.

Who would have thought that a fun and casual discussion with Kevin, on a warm summer evening on our patio, would inspire a new pursuit of knowledge and passion for him to change careers? He knew it was time to put down the work belt at Livingston Corp. and pursue a new career path, since he sensed that he wouldn't be fully embraced to step into his father's company.

Back in Canada, I started helping Kevin at his work with his bookkeeping on Fridays, which gave me a new and welcomed challenge to step into the workforce and still be the primary parent at home with the girls. We concluded, though, that if he was ever going to go back to school to pursue a new career, the time had to be soon while the girls were still young.

At the end of that summer of 2003, amidst the great Okanagan Mountain fires, which destroyed thousands of homes, we decided to visit the Pacific Northwest and check out some of the universities. The anticipation of a new country and a new career was exhilarating and yet a bit fearsome since we would be there with a student visa and not a work visa. Funds would be tight with a family of six.

We packed our motorhome and journeyed on

an adventure to the Pacific Northwest. We enjoyed discovering the oceanside cities, and we'll always remember driving the sand dunes and tumbling down the sand hills by the ocean beach. We gorged on breakfast pancakes and salt-water taffy, and we consumed tubs of locally made ice cream on the side of the road after our motorhome's refrigerator broke down.

After Kevin met with the dean of a university, he was, much to our astonishment, accepted to go to the school at the start of the next semester. That meant he had a couple weeks to pack up after we got back from our investigative vacation, and he'd be on his way to dive into a world of collegiate studies once again.

God was also teaching me a new word alongside *change,* and that word was *faith*. We will be riding under the wings of faith as we return from our motorhome trip of adventure to the Pacific Northwest, but I will have to stay behind in the Okanagan with the girls until our home sells. Then I have the big job of packing everything up, virtually on my own, with four young children to look after. It was quite a task to get our home ready to sell.

Our home sold after three months, and we made the big move to the United States, with the money from our home equity in the bank to transfer to American funds. That was still back in the day when the currency exchange was favorable to Canadians.

We had a freezer full of rye bread and a pocket full of sunshine, sprinkled with seeds of faith to last our next three to four years while Kevin studied at the college. We were embarking on a time of frugal means and enormous faith.

January in Washington brings rain, rain, and more rain, although yesterday, winter visited us for one day and brought a dump of snow. It was so fun to watch the kids having a snowball fight, barricaded by their snow forts. It was Makenna, Brooklyn, Everleigh, and the neighbor boy against Daddy and his ammunition gal, Ellie.

Ellie is sweet and spicy, and I marvel at her musical talent at this young age while I listen to her sing Avril Lavigne's "Chasing down every temporary high," without need of a microphone. This Christmas, at the age of five, she sang us "Silent Night" while Makenna played the piano. It was so sweet, and she sounded like a tiny angelic bird. "Bubbles" is what I call her these days, for she is like a bubble waiting to burst, and their daddy still calls all the girls "Sweet pea."

Of course, some of our favorite times are on a lazy holiday morning when the girls secretly get busy in the kitchen to surprise us with breakfast in bed. On my birthday this last July, before we moved, the girls cleaned up the playroom, set a fancy table by the panoramic window, and even wrote up a fancy menu, decorated with creative love. We enjoyed grapes and toast and juice. What a blessed surprise.

Makenna is proficient with e-mails, and I think she's been e-mailing her first boyfriend, who she misses dearly since they moved apart. The move has been a challenge for her, as she was so sad to leave her friends behind in Canada. It's still good to have her home on Friday nights, and I often see her playing basketball with the neighbor boy. I know she'll grow up far too soon in these next years to come, and I already must accept the conversation of her wondering where she'll get her driver's license, in the USA or Canada.

Ellie just put some laundry in the hamper and noticed some high-heeled shoes of mine. She loves dressing me up and putting lipstick and jewelry on me. So I pause again for a moment to marvel at the white four-inch heels she just strapped on my feet. She never stops telling me how beautiful I am.

Brooklyn is downstairs vacuuming because all the girls just got in trouble, and their daddy was far from happy and far from hugging. Their kitchen cleaning turned into a crying towel fight, so now they only have twenty minutes to clean the entire family room and kitchen. Oh, it's good to be king and queen for a moment, and I'm sure these will be some of the best days of our lives, even if our family of six is living in a rental home that is half the size of our former house in Canada.

These are good days, and forever etched into my mind are those times when I find homework strewn all over the house. I'll tuck away these special treasures like a poem, or story, or an artistic masterpiece, and keep them always. These are moments that can never be replaced.

Through the days of challenges, changes, and adventurous joy, the Lord intends to bring us to a place closer to Him as we pursue righteousness and desire to wear His robe of righteousness.

> Brothers and sisters, I do not consider myself yet to have taken hold of it. But one thing I do: Forgetting what is behind and

straining toward what is ahead, I press on toward the goal to win the prize for which God has called me heavenward in Christ Jesus.

—Philippians 3:13–14

Chapter 21

A WARNING CALL FOR PURITY

The White Wedding Gown Dream: 2007

The other night, I dreamed I was in a clothing store with other young girls. The store owner was so lovely and elegantly dressed. The young girls and I were trying to choose an outfit for a wedding we were all going to attend. One of the girls held up a skimpy lace see-through skirt and asked if she could wear it. I winced with almost humorous disdain and said, "I don't think that dress is quite appropriate." They thought I was old-fashioned.

The store owner wanted to show me the brand-new shipment of dresses that just arrived. I paused for a moment and decided to follow her into the back room of the store. The floor was covered with dust, and I said I thought we should first vacuum the floor before making the room ready for the new racks of wedding gowns.

The store owner then showed me the rack of wedding dresses. Our eyebrows were raised as we took in the sight of these uniquely simple but proper gowns. It was an entire storehouse of pure white cotton dresses that were sewn with many gatherings and brought together with ties. I was quite enamored with the simple purity of the gowns, while the young girls mocked the dresses because they weren't sexy enough to show their figure. I, on the other hand, was a little more open to them. There was a sense of pure coverage, lacking envy and competition. I liked the idea of these new dresses. Surely anyone wearing these dresses would be fit for the most special wedding day.

Upon waking with this dream in mind, I knew God was warning me to make wise choices and help teach my four daughters to become ladies of purity who would be fit to make honorable choices We all need to prepare ourselves, like the Bride of Christ, pure and spotless, ready for "such a time as this," ready for our King, just like in the book of Esther.

It has become so important, especially as a mom with girls entering teen years, that our "yes," would be "yes," and our "no" would be "no," and we need to be eager to do what is good. My dream reminded me that God wanted us to continue having many gatherings with people in the same Christian belief, for these would be the ties that bind us in our faith and love. Christ will one day soon return for His Bride, and we are to be ready in our pure, white, spotless gowns.

I uttered my desire and promise to God, and I remember the sticky note I kept in my Bible to "Do the right thing at the right time for the right reason" and "I will do what I don't want to do to be the person God wants me to be." So, help me God, as I write and teach my girls and their girlfriends.

> Likewise, teach the older women to be reverent in the way they live … then they can urge the younger women … to be self-controlled and Pure.
>
> —1 Titus 2:3–5

And to present her to himself as a radiant church, without stain or wrinkle or any other blemish, but holy and blameless.

—Ephesians 5:27

Chapter 22

THE STRONGHOLD:
SEPTEMBER 2008

When trial, temptation, and grief give way to another stop, another pause that takes you back to the same shock and pain you've experienced in the past, you must consider why you chose to love and vowed to be faithful. We, just like the Israelites who wandered around the desert for forty years, can revisit the same cycle that throws us for another loop. We continue going around and around that same roundabout while forgetting to yield, exit, and make the correct right turn.

Again, it feels like I am sitting in that same old dank

shack of painful hurt, triggered by regret and a spouse's betrayal. I sit here in silent shock, cowering and sobbing in the corner beside the cold toilet, wondering how my dearest friend and love could hurt me again so deeply.

My throat felt clamped, strained, and nearly breathless.

Upon the chance discovery of a love note, I once again confronted Kevin and demanded the truth, but the only thing I got was a backlash of anger for finding the note, while the evidence and words were right in my hands.

The stronghold, instead of owning up to the truth, decides to deflect and make the problem mine. I wasn't supposed to find the note. So, the anger lashes out and attacks and literally tries to choke the breath right out of me. The fear of suffocation and the strength to survive overrides the shock.

Heaven have mercy when your child is around to experience or witness the stronghold. Yet, thank God the cry and shock of your child's reaction could have been what brought the grip's release and your breath back.

The devil only knows how to use a collegiate environment to tempt your loved ones and throw you back into the torrential storm. This is how Satan slithers back in the home and peaceful garden to come between a husband and wife, and the calling God has for you.

You gasp for breath, you cry, and you ask yourself why you even care anymore. You question your being when one says that your efforts don't count, or you don't make a difference. You are broken and shattered.

You choose to shake off this attack, and you wonder how you're going to continue to forgive and love, but you do. You continue for the sake of the family and because you still see the good in the spouse you chose to love. You believe in forgiveness seventy times seven.

These past few years have brought me full circle out of what pain from betrayal means. We all long to be the only one who utters the words, "I love you," to our spouse. We long to be the only one who shares those intimate and loving moments and words with our spouse. New discoveries of deceit and lies come to light and reveal betrayal upon betrayal. Indiscretions become exposed, and we tell the same story again and again.

I promise myself that I will never let a stronghold like that ever demean my self-worth again. We make room for forgiveness and grace, yet there is the strength of the overcomer that pushes you to get back up on the treadmill of life. You insist on becoming someone new and beautiful and loved and respected.

You dye your hair a completely different color, lose twenty pounds, and get a sexy outfit so your husband will notice you and be proud of you. You vow that you will make him take a second look at you as the brilliant and dynamic woman you are. You work hard to study and get that professional career and put that power suit back on and walk tall. You say to yourself that you are a brilliant and tenacious woman, worthy of your husband's love.

Like a man, a woman is created equal, aside from differing strengths, and whatever your calling, both can accomplish great things. Being a stay-at-home mom of four girls is not easy, especially when your husband is an absentee father because he's at school and studying most of the time.

I was trying, and I was working hard. I was helping by doing bookkeeping and painting neighbors' homes, and I was also trying to study for my real estate license while being home for our girls. It was so cruel of Kevin to say what I was doing wasn't making a difference. I know I am a hard worker. I was created on purpose, and even though I may be the weaker vessel, God created me with a mind and a voice, and I can still roar and stand up for righteousness. I hold a strong disdain for what is considered unjust, offensive, abusive, and insulting.

I do not consider myself above anyone else, and I respect men of integrity and honor, and in all humility, I recognize that I too am equally a sinner, yet I can still stand up for truth and integrity.

I am honest, I am open and truthful, and I expect the same from the one I trust to love and protect me and my family. We are all human, and we are all faulty beings. I am also forgiven. If we expect Christ to forgive us, shouldn't we also forgive others? I will leave room for Christ's judgment, but I am just human, and I am indignant.

Beauty from All of This Mess

There's a new story; same story, none can save face,
not one of us innocent, and we all fall from grace.

There's a new face and a new name, new
reason and bait,
but it's all the same story, and we all can
relate.
It's the same through generations with the
elephant in the room, where one speaks
out of turn and one sings out of tune.
We speak not the truth, through mystery
and rhyme,
to save face and save ego in wrong place
and time.
For hurt people, hurt people, that's just
how it is.
It's his story and her story; it's mine and
it's his.
Your story may be similar or even be
worse,
it may start with a blessing and end with
a curse.
Yet for the good of the family, we forgive
and hope best,
and thank God He can make beauty from
all of this mess.

Dear Younger Me,

Forgiveness does heal the painful and open
wounds of betrayal, but this cycle of deception
and pain will one day be successful in squeezing
the life out of you. You thought you left all those
bad experiences and choices behind, yet you
continue to return hurt for hurt. The painful
discovery of that love note brought back the
same lies, confrontation, literal physical abuse
and pain, regret, isolation, and abandonment.
Somehow, in our broken humanity, we must
change directions on that path that exchanges
hurt with hurt. Unaware of the great deceiver
and father of lies, that same cycle of regret can
rear its ugly head over and over again.

I am proud that you overcame those obstacles
through truth and disclosure and were able to
humble yourselves and forgive. Christ's grace
shows up in full repentance and forgiveness.
It's only when we take proper counsel to dig
deep into our hearts to expose and extract
deep roots of selfishness, pride, deception,
lust, unforgiveness, and bitterness, that we can
find true repentance at the foot of the cross.
Have you both really done the needed work

of revealing the truth and digging in deep to remove those deceptive bitter roots? Why is our fallen humanity so daft?

For our struggle is not against flesh and blood, but against the rulers, against the authorities, against the powers of this dark world and against the spiritual forces of evil in the heavenly realms.

—Ephesians 6:12

He has shown you, O mortal, what is good. And what does the Lord require of you? To act justly and to love mercy and to walk humbly with your God.

—Micah 6:8

For if you forgive other people who sin against you, your heavenly Father will also forgive you, but if you do not forgive others their sins, your Father will not forgive your sins.

—Matthew 6:14–15

Do not judge, and you will not be judged. Do not condemn, and you will not be condemned. Forgive, and you will be forgiven.

—Luke 6:37

Pride goes before destruction, a haughty spirit before a fall.

—Proverbs 16:18

Chapter 23

KEEP ON KEEP'N ON: 2006/2008

In 2006, Kevin finished his twelfth year of university and opened his new professional office in the Pacific Northwest. I was his front office manager, and even though we had entered the greatest housing crash in 2008, I still pursued a real estate career.

We lived close to our girls' school and across the street from our church. The girls were involved with Young Life, volleyball, piano, guitar lessons, golf lessons, dance lessons, swim lessons, and after-school programs at their high school. We took the time to go to church on Sundays, loved our Sunday brunches, and enjoyed our favorite five-dollar foot-long Subway sandwiches.

Makenna and Brooklyn were finally able to get their driver's licenses, so we felt the kids were becoming more independent and able to care for themselves a bit more. I was free to spread my wings once again, so I worked with Kevin in his office during the week and pursued my real estate career on the weekends. We pushed ourselves on that treadmill of life and got up at 4:30 a.m. and came home between 7:00 p.m. and 9:00 p.m. We were on the stairway of success and made the most money we had ever made in our life. Those were some of the most profitable, yet exhausting times. Once again, God gave us the grace to forgive and put our regretful memories behind us to love each other, to love life and our girls, and to fly once again.

We were still paying off Kevin's surmounting school debt when Makenna graduated and decided to go to university. With some of my own real estate skills, I managed to make a good business connection so we could buy a new home. Kevin bought a shiny new motorbike, and I bought a shiny black piano with help from my real estate sales. I loved hearing our four musically talented girls play that baby grand piano for us.

Kevin and I finished the interior of our new home as we chose carpet and countertops, and I painted the interior. I even painted our neighbor's home to help with some of the finances. I hauled dirt and picked weeds before laying out turf; I helped build flower beds with rock edge landscaping and dragged around rows of baby cedar trees to plant. I didn't mind working hard until my back ached and felt out of place. I could hardly walk, and it was so painful to move and do work, but I kept on pushing ahead, for there was so much work to be done.

Early one morning at 4:30 a.m., we hustled out the door to get across the bridge to go to the gym before work. The morning was icy cold and sprinkled with frosty snow as I headed out the door onto the wood deck to go down the steps. I was unaware of the invisible sheer ice beneath the frosting of snow on the steps, and my legs slipped out from under me, and I landed right on my tailbone.

Kevin saw me slip and fall; I was in pain. We were late for work, so I tried to get up and managed to walk down the stairs. But I started to feel the blood rush from my head, and the sound in my ears started to fade out to nothing. The last thing I remember, before I blacked out, was Kevin catching me in his arms and laying me down on the icy pavement.

All sound faded into the silence, and the noise was gone.

Everything went black.

I was out, on the ground, for what seemed like a thousand years.

Wait! What?

Was it a thousand years since I was gone, or just a few minutes?

I woke up on the icy pavement and then wondered why Kevin was coming out of the house. Why did he just say, "Come on, let's go, we gotta get to work"?

I was bewildered and wondered, *What just happened? Why didn't he care that I just slipped down the stairs and fell on my tailbone? Did I faint, or what? Is this all a bad dream? I thought he caught me. I can hardly walk. Wasn't that fall a big deal? Why are we rushing to work and not going to the hospital to see if I damaged something?*

Somewhere lost in the days of time, between the choking attack, doing landscaping, or the slip down the steps, an MRI proved that I had a herniated disc. Walking, lifting, sitting, vacuuming, and yard work were now very difficult and painful.

We both continued to work, and the days were a long tough slug, but business was lucrative. By the time 2011 came, we were faced with a decision of choosing the long path to American citizenship or returning to our home country of Canada.

Looking back on our nine years in the United States, our family could undoubtedly agree they were some of the most difficult times, but at the same time, those days were filled with the most special times Kevin and I could remember. We enjoyed carefree weekend motorbike rides on his bike. I loved wrapping my arms around his strong chest as we got out to feel the breeze on our face and smell the fresh scent of the great outdoors as the sights, sounds, and scents of the luscious Pacific Northwest farmland passed us by.

Our girls, on the other hand, would say the great shopping malls of Northwest America were their favorite things. We loved weekend family trips to the ocean and hiking the trails of Silver and Multnomah Falls.

Kevin and I would find the renewed thrill in meeting

for Friday Happy Hour at the local sushi restaurant and escaping for romantic birthday and anniversary experiences at the City Skyview Grill. I would have to say my most endearing and heart-warming experience was the Christmas of 2011, when we planned an outing to the Christmas Lodge in central Oregon. Oh, what a beautiful memory of going on a horse-drawn sleigh ride and drinking hot chocolate by the fireside with our girls.

That Christmas in 2011 captured the happy photos of shared gifts wrapped in shiny big boxes and sweet thank-you kisses. This was one of the dearest times that our family of six shared together. It had been a long time since we experienced a quiet and peaceful Christmas together. Making memories for ourselves without the chaotic travels of visiting the entire extended family was a rare and special gift.

> I know, my God, that you test the heart and are pleased with integrity. All these things I have given willingly and with honest intent. And now I have seen with joy how willingly your people who are here have given to you.
>
> —1 Chronicles 29:17

This day I call the heavens and the earth as witnesses against you that I have set before you life and death, blessings, and curses. Now choose life, so that you and your children may live.

—Deuteronomy 30:19

Chapter 24

THE WAY BACK
HOME: 2012

With a promise and a prayer, we made our way back to Canada. We packed a caravan of vehicles stuffed with furniture and boxed family heirlooms and journeyed back home to British Columbia.

We opened a new office, and again, I worked alongside Kevin and studied to get my BC real estate license. We both worked hard as we started over again and built our new business. We worked together during the week, and I worked in my real estate business during the weekend. Once again, we were back on the rat race of life.

We definitely took on too much by moving into a big and beautiful new home. The house was perfect, and we had enough rooms for all our girls to have their own rooms and for when the ones from out of town came back home to visit. Ellie was in high school, and the three older girls completed their university years and began their own journeys into careers, marriage, and family life.

Funds were tight, but we were focused and determined to continue to work hard, although our situation became more humbling as we realized the house payments were too costly alongside the struggle of starting a new business. After two years of financial struggle, we had to embrace the reality that we had to sell our beautiful new home and find a smaller house we could afford.

Once again, we were on the move, and the boxes and packing tape came out for the twelfth time since being married. Thank goodness I was a Realtor, and we could save on real estate fees. We found a humble yet very comfortable abode we could put a bit of sweat equity into and make our own.

Life was so very good there in that smaller home in the Meadows. We realized that our time here on earth wasn't just about working hard and obtaining the biggest and the best of everything. It's also about enjoying time together and making memories together as a family, even if it was in finding our quaint, smaller, and still comfortable home we could afford.

I quit being a Realtor since I was always exhausted with moving and working two jobs. I worked all week with Kevin, and then most of the weekend, I was helping clients sell or buy homes. I was exhausted running into the brokerage office at midnight on Sundays because time was of the essence to make a deal and have the chance of making more money. I said enough was enough, and we couldn't work every hour of the week, so I quit and just worked for Kevin in his office. Now work was manageable, and it was good. God provided for us, and we worked well together.

Finally, we had a little more time and a little extra money to buy a trailer and embark on our new dream of experiencing the great outdoors and discovering new mountain journeys. We loved our time in that home in the Meadows.

We were tired of moving, and we longed to make this home our forever home, one where the children could come back when they were married with babies of their own. Finally, now that we were in our early fifties, we had a little time and extra money to visit with the grandbabies and do the fun things we longed to do together. We got busy and transformed that home into a trendy and comfortable house, designing the back yard into a flowery, garden oasis with a hot tub and a two-tiered patio deck with evening lights.

We enjoyed sweet barbeques on summer evenings by the hot tub, and the pink floribunda roses and orange lilies that surrounded our back yard were a sensational delight to marvel at God's wonderful creation.

We made plans to finally take our grown girls on a family vacation to Hawaii, just by ourselves, without the entire, extended Livingston family. What a joy that trip was, and the memory of it was one to rival our Mexican trip we took with the girls decades earlier. From the Mexican grass hut family dance when the girls were under ten years old, to the afternoon charcuterie and mai tais on the Hawaiian patio, when the girls were old enough to share an adult drink, I remember the good things where life was beautiful. We were truly blessed in all ways. This was our life; this was us, and we loved it. We loved us. And even though this home in the Meadows was not big or extravagant by any means, I think we felt like we had finally arrived.

Kevin and I loved cooking together and planning our meals for our weekend getaways to the mountains in our trailer. I'd make mealtime lists and make our family favorite, zucchini carrot cake, for morning coffees, and Kevin perfected his Saturday morning eggs Benedict and his Friday night juicy hamburgers.

The girls and I dreamed of planning their beautiful weddings, and I was more than delighted to help with the wedding flowers and wedding favors. We made great memories in that home in the Meadows, and I cherished our conversations and special moments we shared in the hot tub with our morning coffees, and our evenings surrounded by romantic string lights as we sipped our favorite wine. All the work and hardships were well worth the destination of being here. We felt like we finally arrived.

> I know that there is nothing better for people than to be happy and to do good while they live.
>
> —Ecclesiastes 3:12

Chapter 25

BLESSED OR CURSED IN THE VALLEY OF FLOODS: 20018/2019

One Saturday morning in the spring of 2018, while we were still living in the Meadows, Kevin's father came over and commented that he thought we needed a bigger home. It would have been nice to have one more bedroom for when the kids came back home to visit. It would be nice to have nine-foot ceilings instead of eight-foot, and it would be nice to have a fireplace in the living room, but we were quite content here. We were surprised by the comment, yet we both knew how much work it took to renovate the house and landscape our yard so we could have a home we loved. We were happy and content there.

After moving from our last bigger home, we knew what we could afford and what we couldn't afford. Yet, his father encouraged us to engage a Realtor to look for a bigger home and property, saying he would help us out a bit. We were excited but still quite perplexed about the offer to look for a bigger property. We were blessed and content where we were now and weary from moving so many times. We knew we had to be wise and make sure we knew what the financial details were. We experienced a few disappointments with certain promises and miscommunications in the past when it came to family business dealings.

We booked a Realtor to show us some properties that were available on the market and tried to breach the secretly veiled conversation of the portion of our responsibility, compared to the portion of the gift. We told his father what we could afford, and we prodded for more details about what he meant when he offered to help us out a bit.

His father said we needed to have a larger vision, so we looked at the scope of properties he thought was appropriate. I trusted that Kevin and his father were having those affordability and financial discussions. As the saying goes, "It's not easy changing horses in high waters." We needed to be careful not to overextend ourselves. Why are there veiled conversations within family matters? I don't know why, but we went along with the intrigue of expanding our horizons.

One property we saw seemed veiled in secrecy; it was mysterious and lacking in open honesty. After viewing and carefully considering the property, Kevin and I said the home was just too big for us and the acreage demanded too much time and work for the stage of life we were in, now that all the kids had left home.

I had been a Realtor in previous years, and we discussed a few red flags about the property that were of concern. The age, size, and visual facts of the home revealed characteristics we didn't want to contend with. We knew about acreage and farm work, and that was not something we thought we could handle now that we were in our fifties and embarking on our retirement years.

Both Kevin and I agreed and said, "No, sorry, that's not the property for us."

Two days later, we arranged to see a smaller

property we thought we would like. After looking at the property with the Realtor and Kevin's parents, we sat alone with his parents in our car and asked what they thought about this property.

His father paused and then answered, "I'm done with you kids. You're on your own."

Kevin's mom remained quiet, and we were quietly in shock with his answer. We were without words from his father's reply. We hadn't asked for his help to buy a new home, and we hadn't asked for any money from his parents. We were absolutely astonished by the harsh reply. Kevin and I looked at each other with a puzzled look and chose to drive back to his parents' house in silence.

After dropping Kevin's parents off at their home, we both vowed that we would never allow his father to manipulate us and coerce us into doing something we didn't want to do. We said if we ever wanted to move, we would do it on our terms and to a property we chose. We concluded we would not play a game like that ever again. We were embarrassed for wasting our Realtor's time and apologized to her, saying our plans fell through and we couldn't move at this time. Both Kevin and I were upset with how his father reacted and how he had a way of exerting his influence, control, and manipulation on our lives when, as husband and wife, we should have made our own decisions.

We always appreciated any wise counsel his parents could give us, and we wanted to honor them in what they thought we should do. We felt a huge pressure to please his father and obey all his family wanted us to do, whether it was in business dealings or family vacations. His father's business was successful, and God blessed him financially, and we were very grateful for any gifts he gave us and our children over the years, but we were confused with the mysteries, the unspoken words, the miscommunications, the control, and lack of disclosure.

The family secrets and unspoken words became, in my point of view, flat-out lies and deception. We both were baffled and confused, but we continued to respect them and invited his parents and his sister's family for Mother's Day brunches on the patio and candlelit dinners on family celebrations and holidays.

We went back to our home in the Meadows and continued life as we knew it then and there. We enjoyed the blessings of what we did have instead of dreaming of something more, bigger, and supposedly better. We were still blessed and content.

It was early spring of 2018, and we started spring clean-up in our yard; we pruned our perennial flowering shrubs, planted our colorful annual petunias, and even started a small vegetable garden with sweet strawberries and an abundance of heirloom, Early Girl, Brandy Wine, and Mortgage Lifter tomatoes. On the weekends, we would pack up our trailer and get excited about the fresh forest walks and campfires in the evening.

We worked hard together in Kevin's office during the week, and when we weren't planning weekend getaways, we'd attend our church on Sundays. We even started leading a young couple and facilitated their marriage preparation course. We had come through a lot of marriage issues of our own in the past and saw some of our own children through the marriage and wedding process, and we saw what a marriage centered around God and Christian morals and choices could do to help a marriage bloom into a blessed union. We felt God's calling into this marriage ministry.

Three of our four daughters were married during our time living in the Meadows, and our first grandbaby was also born at that time. We had wedding and baby showers at that home and gathered for Christmas celebrations. Ellie played our grand piano and her guitar, recorded music, and we celebrated our joys and accomplishments. Our children had wonderful careers, boyfriends, and husbands, and we were proud of them and couldn't wait to have them come back home to visit us. Love was in the air, and future excitement was on the horizon as we planned and celebrated and dreamed together.

Eight months later, in December of 2018, I hosted an intimate family dinner party and invited Kevin's parents. Towards the end of the evening, Kevin's father made a statement, saying, "I bought that large acreage property on the hill, and if you want to buy it from me for a good deal, you can, or I'll rent it out to someone else." He also added that he started to build a barn on it.

We were puzzled and shocked all at the same time and did not know how to respond. Although we were incredibly grateful for this seemingly huge gift and opportunity, we were taken aback because we had told him six months ago that we didn't want that property, and he said he was done with helping us kids. We didn't want to dishonor our parents by looking a gift horse in the mouth, so we said we would think about it and talk it over together. We should have prayed and asked God what to do. Really, in hindsight, we should have prayed about it together, as husband and wife.

Kevin and I were in shock, but quite excited about this opportunity and gift. We were baffled at how this all unfolded and the lack of our involvement. At the same time, we were overwhelmed with the idea of this huge gift. We were grateful for his father's offer, which seemed to be cloaked in our inheritance gift. How could we refuse such a gift, and how could we not be thankful for the offer? We knew the property was more than we could handle, but we were grateful for the opportunity, and we said, "Okay, yes, thank you."

Once again, for the third time in six years, we made plans to move and got excited about the idea of having an acreage and a dream barn. We'd make the best of this incredible gift. We discussed the financial responsibilities and knew what portion we could afford for the property.

We signed the real estate documents, including the gift portion document, and his father had his purchase contract assigned over to us. We didn't question him. We trusted him, for he was our father. We were excited and thought we would work hard and make the best of it. We could handle the acreage work for about the next five years or so, until we were in our early sixties.

We were excited to show the girls when they came home over the Christmas holidays. We didn't even have a second look at the property, and we really didn't remember what the house looked like anymore, but for the video the listing agent still had up from when it was listed.

Being a Realtor in the past, I wondered how that deal went down and wondered about the delay in us finding out about his father buying the property and why the contract didn't have Realtors mentioned. I knew about contract law, and I knew about disclosures, and I knew about commissions due to Realtors, and I knew about the importance of home inspections, but the deal and paperwork seemed to be void of any of those details of due diligence. Both Kevin's and my name were on the gift letter and the assignment of the contract. We both signed the real estate contract, even though there seemed to be odd comments and undisclosed secrets that we weren't privy to. We really didn't know how the original purchase was completed and processed since we had only seen the property once, six months prior.

In early spring of 2019, after most of the snow was melted, the boxes were once again unpacked, and after we moved into the house, it still felt like there was a cursed, dark veil, and cloud of secrecy that hovered over our new home, because of the process in which it was purchased. I felt like Kevin and I were the last to know about our own home purchase, and we had no real say in the matter. We felt coerced and manipulated, and frankly, we were exhausted and tired of working, packing up, and moving so many times. I tried to hide my discontent for how our life was unfolding and the revelation of truth now being exposed through puzzling conversation, yet we pressed on and hoped for exciting times ahead of us.

Both Kevin and I took the stand of respecting and honoring his parents, and being thankful, and making the best of our new situation. I told myself, "What doesn't kill us makes us stronger." We were confident that we could stay strong and do our best to work together to make something very good out of this new home and acreage, but we weren't prepared for the stormwaters that came in the valley of floods.

> Even though I walk through the darkest
> valley, I will fear no evil, for you are with me;
> your rod and your staff, they comfort me.
> —Psalm 23:4

Chapter 26

ABSENCE OF FULL DISCLOSURE: SPRING OF 2020

When secret deceptions hide latent behind the walls of dishonesty, the walls are bound to come tumbling down, and the exposure of truth unfolded before our eyes. New evidence emerged as hidden things were not disclosed.

Our physical home and calamities on our property reflected what was happening in the trial for our marriage in the spiritual realm. Our home and property experienced flood after flood, water pipes made from flimsy Polly B snapped, and burst forth flood waters.

The clay mud and soil our home foundation was built on started to slip, only to reveal previously separated cement foundation posts. Our decks and stairs slipped away, and cracks popped up all over the place. We were so upset that we had to deal with all this chaos and turmoil. We put our trust in others to make wise decisions on our behalf. We knew that purchasing this property went against our first and better judgment, but we persevered through the work.

I discovered later, through the demand of legal disclosures, that the original purchase of our home and property was managed in a shady manner, and all the secret deals made behind closed doors were now becoming unequivocally obvious to the naked eye. Since I was previously a Realtor, I was upset at myself for not asking the right questions and for putting my trust in others to make wise decisions on our behalf.

We were battling in our earthly realm, and storms were brewing in the spiritual realm of our marriage. These were the problems that can arise when we put our trust in man, money, and the things of this earthly world. We were overwhelmed with two floods in our home; the devastating workload and cost to repair our home were insurmountable.

We chose not to point fingers, since we also didn't ask the right questions, and we didn't let our "No" be "No, thank you, but thank you for your kind offer." We kept our complaints to ourselves and chose to work hard and put a smile on our faces to still honor and respect his parents. I put my big girl pants on, and we put on our work gloves and started repairing our home and rebuilding our dream. We scooped up buckets of water, we glued pipes, we dug out from under the clay, we ripped out walls and carpets, and we tried to restore our belongings. We rebuilt, worked hard, repaired, and replanted.

We started to see the light and started to dream again. We grew flowers and vegetables in the garden and made homegrown salads and homemade vegetable soups. I made a cut flower garden and created beautiful floral and bridal bouquets, and I gave away flower arrangements to friends and family. We shared our strawberries and gave away huge homegrown zucchinis. We were blessed and enjoyed harvest and Christmas at home celebrations.

> But the one who hears my words and does not put them into practice is like a

man who built a house on the ground without a foundation. The moment the torrent struck that house, it collapsed and its destruction was complete.

—Luke 6:49

A good person leaves an inheritance for their children's children, but a sinner's wealth is stored up for the righteous.

—Proverbs 13:22

Chapter 27

BEWITCHED DESCENT:
FEBRUARY 2023

I often dream at night when I was asleep, but I've only heard the audible voice of God on two occasions. One night, I was awakened by a powerful, yet gentle, man's voice saying one word: "Legacy." The other time was when that same authoritative voice woke me with two words: "Fly, Alive." It seems now that these three words God gave me were going to be the forerunners that would lead me with courageous strength, meaningful purpose, and unrestrained faith.

The Holy Spirit is reminding me this battle belongs to the Lord, and I must change my thinking about who my enemy is. This battle rages within my heart and mind as I hold onto anger, bitterness, and hate towards the people who betrayed and hurt me. I know I must let go of my past hurts and wounds from my husband and the people who got in between our marriage, and I must repent of my hate, bitterness, and anger and ask the Lord to forgive me as I continually forgive those who have hurt and betrayed me. It's a daily process of surrendering all to Jesus.

The Lord has also shown me my husband was deceived by Satan. Satan leads people astray by evil spirits, and the enemy that slipped into our life and home came from the demonic realm. My battle is not with these people who hurt and rejected me, but my battle is with the demonic, spiritual realm. This attack is one that must be fought with the sword of the spirit, in God's Word, and by prayer and fasting.

Many of these demonic strongholds come through sins and bloodlines of the fathers, mothers, and grandparents. Unless we rebuke and take authority over these generational curses and familiar spirits, by the power and blood of Jesus Christ, we will continue to allow those evil spirits to throw our family into trials and strife. I undoubtedly knew that all I was experiencing through these past years and this great separation and chaotic turmoil was because of open doors that allowed the familiar spirits to sneak into our home and marriage. These strongholds can come in through witchcraft, spells, curses, and evil strongholds that come in through poor choices of alcohol abuse, drugs, pornography, lust, unholy relationships, greed, and deceptive lies.

These demonic strongholds that destroy individuals, marriages, families, and homes can be passed down through generations of family members who've dabbled in the occult, sexual sins, and evil practices through deceptive lies and manipulative control. Manipulation is a form of witchcraft. Some of these demonic strongholds even lurk around as wolves in sheep's clothing in the Christian church. I've seen pastors fall and Christian leaders' marriages and families destroyed by the sneaky deception and lure of temptation. Satan is our real enemy; he wants to kill us and destroy us, and he'll do this in any way he can. He'll pull the wool over any weak sheep's eyes if we don't have our eyes open to the truth.

Whether we intended for these demonic strongholds to enter our life or not, somehow, we let them into our relationships, our home and family, and our marriage. I do believe that curses can be passed down through continued sins of the forefathers, and family bloodlines from grandparents, and continue to tempt and destroy families for generations to come, unless we stop them through prayer, fasting, and true repentance. We have authority over the enemy with the power, the blood, and the name of Jesus Christ.

Again, some of these demonic spirits can slip through open doors by

- control and manipulation,
- selfish desires and pursuits of this world,
- greed and lust of the flesh,
- greed for power and money,
- addiction, pornography, fornication, and sexual misconduct,
- unholy thoughts and practices,
- unholy entertainment and music, lyrics, blasphemy, and cursing,
- lies, deceit, betrayal, and chaotic confusion,
- illegal activity and abuse, and
- pagan practices, witchcraft, occults, and new age practices.

I know that right now, I am called to pray and fast for the deliverance and redemption of my family and marriage. Whether God has a plan to return my husband back, restored and redeemed through a softened heart of repentance and love, first for God, or whether I must continue walking this new road alone with God and without Kevin, I don't know. This one thing I know: We must be set free from the evil that caused destruction in our relationship.

I think back to the dream I had a few months before I became aware of the betrayal and when Kevin said he wanted a divorce. I had these two dreams in 2018 and 2019 when I became aware of the other woman who was coming between my husband and me.

The Girl with the Tattoo Dream, 2018

I had a dream that I was at our work front desk, ready to process the next billing for the person who was seeing Kevin for an appointment. In my dream, I saw lewd images of a naked woman floating around in the office room where Kevin was with the door locked. Then I saw a girl come out of the office. She looked familiar, but I couldn't put a name to her. Her hair was long and black, and she had a tattoo on her left, back shoulder.

When I woke up, I was troubled and disturbed at what I had dreamt, and I couldn't imagine this woman was anyone I knew. Maybe she was just a metaphor.

The Python and Goat Dream, 2019

In 2019, I dreamt I was sitting on our big, comfy, family room chair Kevin always chose to sit on. He'd often sit in that chair and scroll through his iPad, or relax and have a glass of whiskey or scotch as he'd unwind from a long day of work.

In the dream, I was sitting on Kevin's big, comfy chair, and I felt an enormous pressure on top of me. The pressure was from a giant black python that was coiled up on top of my lap. The snake was extremely heavy, and the weight was all consuming, but it was on my lap, and I wasn't in its squeezing coil.

There was a black-and-white goat entangled in the python's squeeze, pressing the life out of the bleating goat. I wanted to pull the goat out from the snake, but I couldn't get the goat released. I had the goat by the ears to pull it free, but I couldn't release the stronghold, and the tugging only caused the goat's face to split in two, exposing its raw flesh. Then I woke.

These dreams were troubling and concerned me. They were warnings of strongholds, trials, and tribulations that were going to put a tremendous squeeze and pressure on my marriage and life over the next couple of years. I knew I needed to go into the throne room of grace for prayer for Kevin, myself, and our marriage.

> For our struggle is not against flesh and blood, but against the rulers, against the authorities, against the powers of this dark world and against the spiritual forces of evil in the heavenly realms.
>
> —Ephesians 6:12

Be strong and courageous. Do not be afraid or terrified, for the Lord your God goes with you; he will never leave you nor forsake you.

—Deuteronomy 31:6

Chapter 28

THE DARK ALLEY OF FEAR: SPRING 2020

All the chaotic events seemed to collide within the same month and even the same week in the spring of 2020. We were faced with the lockdowns and stress of COVID shutdowns. Our business was sinking fast like the *Titanic* in frozen waters. We had no other choice but to move our business to our outbuilding at our home location.

We had two floods in our home, and then a huge and unexpected tax bill was dropped off, in an envelope. That was the same night when Kevin had a heart attack.

We had no idea this tax bill was coming, and the

heart attack to follow was overwhelming. We were afraid. Kevin woke me up at 1:00 a.m. and asked me to drive him to the hospital, because he knew he had been experiencing the first signs of having a heart attack for the past two hours. He tried to rest quietly so I wouldn't wake up and he wouldn't alarm me, but it became all too real and all too pressing.

It was a long wait in the emergency room that night, as he had heart monitors and leads hooked up to his chest. But God was good. Kevin's blood vessels had collapsed and he had a heart attack, but the area wasn't crucial to his health. The blood took a different pathway that bypassed the dead veins. He was blessed and lucky to hardly have an interruption to the quality of his life. Thank God he would be okay with the right medication. Literally, a small part of his heart died that day.

In the early summer of 2020, I had another significant dream. I was in an unfamiliar city that looked like San Francisco. It was an eerie atmosphere at dusk, the time of day when light was growing dim. I stood between high-rise buildings in a dark, dank alley, where sewage ran openly, and painted profanity and graffiti was sprayed on the cracked walls of the buildings that surrounded me.

I saw Kevin in the middle of the alley, about fifty feet away from me. He was wearing his semi-formal blazer he often wore to church and his casual jeans and brown shoes he wore to work. Within his faraway distant gaze, I saw a detached, yet panicked look of fear, and then he turned from looking at me and ran down the dark alley. I was left there, feeling totally abandoned, scared, and in a state of crisis of being alone and not knowing where I was. As he ran as fast as he could away from me, I realized a young, hooded man was running after him and trying to chase him down.

Still in the same dream, I was suddenly transported to a different place on a steep cliff and mountain of jagged-edged stone, overlooking a dark, bottomless abyss. Then I woke with breathless fear.

After a moment, I caught my breath and turned to Kevin, as he was just waking as well. I exhaled in relief to see he was there, and his presence brought me back to feeling comforted.

"Good morning," I said to Kevin as we both woke up; it was around seven o'clock.

I was still restless and stressed by the dream I had a few moments ago.

"You would not believe the dream I just had," I

continued as he was stretching from his slumber. I told him about my dramatic dream and didn't leave any detail out, for the image of the dream was still etched in my mind.

> Blessed is the one who perseveres under trial because, having stood the test, that person will receive the crown of life that the Lord has promised to those who love him.
>
> —James 1:12

> But he was pierced for our transgressions, he was crushed for our iniquities; the punishment that brought us peace was on him, and by his wounds we are healed.
>
> —Isaiah 53:5

> In that day, I will restore David's fallen shelter. I will repair its broken walls and restore its ruins and will rebuild it as it used to be.
>
> —Amos 9:11

Chapter 29

STILL ROMANCE IN REST AND WORK: SUMMER 2020

"You have wild dreams," Kevin replied after I told him about the dream where he ran away from me in the dark alley.

He stretched under his cover. He rolled over to where I lay, and we found comfort in our cradled cuddle and the morning awakening our entwined bodies. I felt safe; I felt loved and protected. I didn't want to ever leave this place of peace, with Kevin holding me close.

"Come on," he said, stirring us back to reality. "We should get up; we've got to bring the irrigation pipes from the bottom of the hill up to the top of the hay field before I start work in the office."

There was another day of work to be done, starting with changing the sprinkler pipes on the hay field and then watering the greenhouse and vacuuming his office before his appointments started rolling up the driveway of our business, now located in the barn on our property.

We both put on our work clothes and went to the garage to put on our rubber work boots. It was another beautiful and vibrant summer morning, and the hot sun of the day was sure to dry out the field of hay we grew for cattle and horse feed. It was 7:00 a.m., and we had two hours before our day was to start in the office in our barn, located down by my large cut flower garden I planted. Kevin drove the John Deere tractor with the front lift loaded with the sprinkler pipes from the bottom of the field to the top of the field.

I struggled with the desire to have a lazy morning sleep-in, yet the fresh air and the scent of the morning dew on the orchard grass and blue flowering alfalfa was exhilarating to my senses. These were like our early morning dates. It was as if we were in perfect synchronicity in knowing the routine with an all-knowing step and an unspoken song. It was like our dance together in the hay field. We knew the song, and we knew the dance, and we kept in sync. It was our work, but it seemed like our play date.

The routine of changing the sprinkler pipes began with Kevin carrying the heavier and longer pipes in an alternate sequence with me connecting my shorter pipe to his. It was a forty-minute dance to the rhythm of our rubber boots swishing through the alfalfa and orchard grass. We worked in tune with the morning dove coos and the thrusts of the water spraying through the sprinkler heads. The work was fun and seemingly effortless as we knew our next step to complete the refreshing task in tandem. I linger in that memory. I still feel it and hear it and smell the freshness of the air.

The acreage farm days were a lovely memory on that property in the valley. We loved our morning coffees in the hot tub and nurturing our flower and pepper seedlings in the greenhouse. I can still feel the warm morning humidity and see the filtered sun dawning through the greenhouse by the flower garden. We shared so much excitement together, doing our work and fulfilling our dreams of having some land. Regardless of the floods, the turmoil, and the heart attack, we made something beautiful out of it all, and we felt blessed to finally have the land to be able to grow the flowers and vegetables we loved.

> I press on toward the goal to win the prize for which God has called me heavenward in Christ Jesus.
>
> —Philippians 3:14

> God is not unjust; he will not forget your work and the love you have shown him as you have helped his people and continue to help them.
>
> —ΩHebrews 6:10

Chapter 30

DECEPTION INTERSECTION: FALL 2021

How do you put ink on paper and write the beginning of the end of a beautiful love story that's stuck in the ashes of the fires of deception? At the stop in the road and from the center of this mid-life crisis and betrayal, we try to make sense of our beginning and figure out how we got here and where we go next. I really don't know how we'll come out on the other side of this tragic mountain of grief. God only knows what we've been through and if there is a new beginning for us or not. This place of separation and dark night of the soul challenges us to conquer our fears and confusion; we must choose rightly. As I pray to God, I ask where this painful path will lead us, and I wonder if Kevin is still praying. God, has he run so far away from You as well, like the Prodigal Son in the Bible story? Is my husband at this intersection of life and tormented by the decision of having to choose between a false deception or a path of truth?

I hear the Lord answer me, "Yes, My dear. In your dream, where Kevin ran away from you, you never realized that I was always standing right behind you, and that Kevin was running away from Me, from God, and you were just in the middle of us." God continued to reveal this truth to me that Kevin was also running from the young man in the hood, representing that his manhood was chasing him, as in a midlife crisis. God needed to set me aside for a minute, His minute and not my minute, so Kevin would see God clearly and hear His calling for himself, without me in the way.

I feel like Kevin and I are like two rivers that will soon merge on the same path and come together once again; maybe, maybe not? I don't know the future.

My husband, my love,

You were my song, my laughter, my tears, and the one that took my breath away on so many levels. I still have faith, and I still have hope and love in these times of uncertainty. We stop at this big 'X' crossroads of uncertainty, we ask the big 'Y,' and at night, we wrestle with 'ZZZs'. Which way should we go? Should we veer left, or should we stop a little longer to wait and consult the original map which leads us in the right direction? You've run away from me; you've rejected and abandoned me, and although you have free will to choose to run away, I have no say in your choice. For now, you are gone, and I can't force you to come back home to me. My heart aches, and my soul is overwhelmed with grief and loneliness. I miss you, my best friend and soulmate.

November 2021

"Oh, what a beautiful morning, oh, what a beautiful day, I've got a wonderful feeling, everything's going my way." I woke up with this song in my heart and mind this morning as I opened my eyes to a new day at 6:00 a.m. I have no pain coming from the gaping hole where my broken tooth, that exposed such tremendous root and nerve pain, once was. The pillow and empty space beside me are still vacant, and I am alone, except for Jesus giving me a song to wake up to this new morning.

Kevin was still gone, and now so was my tooth. The crack in my tooth caused such an incredible nerve pain that presented like birthing pains. It was excruciating. I went to the dentist to get it pulled yesterday, and now, the absence of my molar left a gaping hole in my gums and became an ironic simile for the hole and emptiness Kevin left beside my pillow, where we once both rested together. Today, my pain was gone.

Many of my pains are now gone. I've prayed and given my pains to Jesus, and now that my life is at this stop and pause, I no longer have all the work I used to have in my life. The pain in my arms and shoulders from all the vacuuming, washing floors and toilets, and sanitizing every surface in Kevin's office, is now gone; my menopausal hot flashes are gone, my pain in my back is gone, and the pain in my ... well, you-know-what is gone. It's good to have a little thought of humor back, even though I can only chuckle to myself. I touch the teddy soft pillow I replaced with Kevin's pillow to comfort me as I slept alone. I think about the times we'd wake up laughing about the silly things we'd say and the play on words that brought humor. I rejoice this morning in this absence of pain, and I embrace this new freedom. Even if this freedom is against my will, and only for Kevin's will or God's will that I am alone, I will bask in this quiet time and lean into the presence of God to be alone with Him, for today, I have much to be thankful for.

The Fireplace Dream: January 2021

In the beginning of the New Year, in early January 2021, I woke up with yet another dream. I wondered why I was having so many dreams at this time of my life. I've shared my dreams, and I was a dreamer. I knew the Holy Spirit spoke to me, warned me, and guided me through my dreams, but my dream life was particularly active these days. Last night, I dreamed there was a beautiful white fireplace, quite like the white fireplace and mantel we had, but more beautiful and purer white. A white billiards ball with an "8" on it rolled across the white mantel then crossed down through the flames in the fireplace and rolled out through the opposite end of the hearth. The pool ball came out the other end just as white, untouched, and unscathed from the fire. Then I woke up.

I pondered what this dream meant, and I shared it with Kevin. This was just another one of my mysterious dreams, and I was alerted and led by the Holy Spirit to question the meaning of this dream.

As I ran my bath water, God revealed the meaning to me. The white mantel represented God's covering over me and the flames and fires of life. God was showing me He would bring me through the coming fires unscathed and untouched by the flames, just like Shadrach, Meshach, and Abednego went through the fires unscathed, with Jesus by their side. The white represented purity and making pure choices, and the 8 ball represented new beginnings. I was concerned, while in the covering and protection of God, that I would be going through the burning and refining fires of trial. God showed me in this dream that I won't be harmed when I come through to the other side. This understanding of my dream strengthened me and gave me hope for what was to come.

During our morning coffee that day, I told Kevin I thought we should plan a trip this weekend to go to Alberta to help Makenna. She was now thirty-one and married and going through a very difficult time. She was going through some losses, had some health issues, and needed help with her sweet one year-old, our granddaughter. Makenna and her husband were also moving the next weekend. She truly needed our help. Kevin agreed, and we discussed plans to travel together to Alberta and help her.

The next day at work, Kevin booked me a flight by myself, without talking with me. He was sending me to Makenna's alone. I was puzzled and confused.

"What?" I exclaimed. "You booked a flight for me alone, and you didn't discuss this change with me first? I thought we were both planning to go together. Makenna needs your help too."

This didn't sit well with me; it triggered me like all the other times he would send me away, alone with our girls. Something bad always happened after I'd come back home. I didn't like it when he made those decisions and forced me to go away by myself on long trips without him. He would push family time and parental responsibilities aside so he could have time alone by himself or with another woman. Things always went sideways when I returned, and this experience was a similar trigger of bad memories.

The next weekend, I went by myself to visit Makenna. I helped her pack, looked after our grandbaby, and did whatever I could do to help her through her stressful time. What a sweet blessing our little nine-month-old granddaughter is, and I wished Kevin could be there to help and get to know his grandbaby more.

The night before flying back home, I couldn't sleep. I was frustrated and anxious because I was so tired and unsettled. It was 3:00 a.m. I decided to look on my cell phone and perused through our social media accounts. I read some of Kevin's posts and noticed flirty exchanges and comments he had with girls I didn't even know. The posts disturbed me. There were so many red flags that came to my mind, and I thought it was strange how he sent me away again by myself instead of coming with me. I pondered his odd behavior from just a couple weeks ago as well. Events reeled through my head from the past month.

Two weeks earlier, one day after work, I had just finished making supper and cleaning the dishes. I decided to finally sit down after the long day to watch some COVID-related news.

Kevin walked by me in a rush as he headed for the garage and abruptly said, "Things are going to change around here. I'm going to start spending more time by myself."

I was dumbfounded and puzzled by that declaration. I couldn't believe he said that so abruptly, and it wasn't like he didn't take time for himself. He would go to visit his dad for lunch by himself, and he would meet his friend at the shooting range by himself. He would go on fishing trips without me and run errands away from me and do volunteer projects by himself. I wasn't sure why he said this. Was this another red flag warning me that something was not right, and I needed to pay attention?

I knew we worked together, but it wasn't like I wanted to get away from him, and I never thought he wanted to get away from me. I was confused about this statement, and it almost sounded like a way to create an alibi. Was I thinking about this too hard and being overly suspicious with this new announcement?

I replied, "Uh, okay?" with a puzzled look on my face as he walked into the garage. I was unsettled by his peculiar behavior, and my world felt out of sorts.

I was upset that morning when I flew back from Alberta. The night before, while still at McKenna's, I sent Kevin a text, and when he picked me up from the airport, we drove home with a strangely uncomfortable conversation about how my time was helping Makenna. After reading my text, he knew I was upset. I told him I wasn't happy about his flirty posts and the peculiar way he was acting lately, and I wasn't happy that he sent me away alone, without consulting me.

When I got home, I looked in the fridge and saw a bunch of strange food in it. There was food that he didn't like and things he'd never let me buy from the store.

"Did you have someone over while I was gone?" I asked.

"No, why do you ask?"

"Because there's a bunch of weird food in the fridge that you've never liked to eat before. Are you sure? Did you have someone over while I was gone?"

He got angry and said, "No, can't a guy try some new things?"

He started getting mad at me about questioning him and the text I had sent earlier. He left the room, and I was worried. I felt as though my world was unravelling.

I started to go upstairs to unpack my suitcases and noticed the formal living room, which we rarely ever sat in. I had vacuumed our plush carpet the evening before I left, and everything was very clean. Now the carpet had footprints pressed into the plush, the pillows were pressed in the chairs, the piano seat was set in a crooked way, and drink coasters were out of place. We never sat in the living room, and he didn't play piano. We always hung out in the family room unless our kids were home. There was every evidence that he had lied, and he did have someone in our house while I was gone for the weekend. I quietly went about my day and didn't want to press anymore of his hot buttons. I was way too exhausted from my busy weekend and lack of sleep.

February 2021

It was almost Valentine's Day, and I had a ton of work to accomplish and get done. The roses and flowers were going to arrive on Thursday, and I had fifteen Valentine's flower arrangements to make for wives of friends. I had to work with Kevin in his office all week as well as sanitizing the COVID out of every touchpoint. The workload was a bit overwhelming. There was so much to do, and I was too tired and too busy for the discovery and revelation that was about to unfold.

There were so many red flags, and then there were the astonishing discoveries. The secrets and lies were exposed. Kevin did have someone over for supper when I was out of town. The betrayal and deflection were followed by the confusing gaslighting he reacted with. I caught him and the other woman crossing professional boundaries, and our sacred marriage relationship was now looking very different. The deception was so upsetting and heartbreaking. For over a decade now, I thought our marriage was on solid ground and we had restored trust.

God sees everything we do, and God will convict each one of us. My story of betrayal may be different from another person's story, but all I know is that it comes down to the severance of the heart and slicing down to the soul and flesh of a husband and wife's covenant relationship. There is unspeakable pain. Lies were told, promises weren't kept, lust crept in, and boundaries were crossed. Whether it's a physical affair or an emotional affair, the beautiful bond of forever friends and lovers, parents, and now grandparents was torn asunder with the lies, the betrayal, and the cold-hearted declaration of, "I want a divorce. I don't love you anymore. Why don't we just be friends with benefits, and why don't you just go out and have an affair too?"

What on earth? Did he really say those things? My mind spiraled as I stood perplexed in this new unearthing and the sting of his words. I cannot wrap my mind around who this man was. Was he living two lives: one for me and the public, and one for her? I cannot make sense of his double-mindedness. How did we go from the happy, mature couple at church, where we mentored young couples through their pre-marriage year, to betrayal, abuse, and divorce?

But, but, wait. What? I thought we were everything to each other. I thought we had it all. I thought we were embarking on a new chapter of being retired grandparents who were still young enough to finally have fun and enjoy the fruits of our labor. I did not want this. I did not want a divorce. I wanted my husband back. Where did he go?

My past collided with my present, and once again hearts were broken, teardrops fell, and families were torn apart. Was 2022 the conclusion and ending of our love story, where separation rips two hearts apart, where properties are divided, and once again, upon confronting the evidence of lies, push comes to shove?

With the risk of sacrificing my comfy complacency in this cozy, lukewarm nest, and knowing there are consequences from sparking the passionate fires of the heart, I decided to stand my ground and confront him for the truth.

It'll start or it'll end here. I consider what it's going to take to reconcile this enormous shortage and loss. Is this my will, is this his will, or is this God's will that will be done here? What's it going to take to repair this inequity of love and lies? If we are calling ourselves Christians in covenant marriage, should we not live in honesty, truth, and integrity? When do we stand up and say, "Enough is enough"? How could my husband stray so far that he would come between our own marriage and another man's marriage? Should a Christian not seek some truth and justice here, or should I just turn the other cheek? We are at this great crossing of truth and hanging on the tipping point of this precipice of deception.

Shut Down, Locked Down, Locked Out: March 2021

After discovering what was really going on in Kevin's office, he pushed me out of our workplace and locked me out of his office and front desk position, where I always assisted him. I was his wife for thirty-four years, and I was his work partner for the past twenty-one years. Besides the hurt and shock of my discovery of his relationship with this other woman and his unprofessional conduct, he abruptly dismantled my job, my dreams, my world, our family, our home, and our marriage. But for some reason, I still wanted him back. I still loved him, and that was very confusing and very perplexing.

I thought he loved me, and I thought we worked so well together. I thought we were in a new place and time, and now living the dream just before the age of retirement. This was our world, this was our work, this was our property, and this was our life and marriage together. How could someone else come between us? How could Kevin lie and deceive me so deeply? How deep did this betrayal and deception go?

"Why? Why are you doing this to me?" I cried out to Kevin.

He stopped and looked confused as he sought the right words and then replied, "You're making me choose between you and my family."

"What are you even talking about? This has nothing to do with your family, and everything to do with what you're doing with Tonya. You're deflecting what's really going on here, and you know I've found out about your lies. I've caught you both in your selfish, lustful deception. You've crossed professional boundaries and marriage boundaries in so many ways here, and now you're blaming me for not getting along with your family? How could you project your wrongdoings onto me? All I've ever done is help you and love you. I just had your family over supper last week. You've agreed that your family has controlled us and manipulated us and kept secrets from both of us. Things went down very badly with the purchase of this property two years ago, and the floods brought us overwhelming work, but we both got over it and we made the best of it here. Why are you even blaming me and doing this?"

"I can't do this anymore," he said. "I'm done. I want a divorce."

I slumped to the ground and cried, "What do you mean, you can't do 'this' anymore? What even is 'this'?"

"Maybe we can just be friends with benefits," he said coldly.

I could not believe what was coming out of his mouth. "Who even are you? How could you even say, 'friends with benefits'? That's disgusting. I'm your wife."

There are no words to describe this broken feeling and emotional trauma that lingers like a trigger of bad memories from what I experienced that day back in February 2021. I despised the discussion of divorce. I despised my husband for saying those words. I despised the other woman, and yes, I despised all the people who got in between us. I despised that I had no say in this matter, and I despised that I was losing everything I loved and worked hard for over the years. I hate divorce, and I felt dead.

How could this be happening, when just a few weeks earlier, we were laughing and loving each other and sharing candlelit dinners together? We were renovating the house from the floods and fixing bedrooms with beds and new comforters for when the kids and grandchildren would come to visit.

We had just gone to the toy store together, feeling like young parents again, but this time we were grandparents, picking out birthday presents for our granddaughter. I remember after a long day of working together, we'd end the day by saying, "Good job," and giving each other a "Knucks to Buddy" cheer, but now, I was devastated by this push out and lock-down that my husband, friend, and partner I loved and worked with for so many years forced upon me. I should be throwing him out for lying and cheating on me, but I don't want him to go; I don't want a divorce.

I still hear the echo of the lock on the barn door clank down as he slammed shut the door that separated his workspace from my flower shop. This was our home-based office we both designed and built together. I was the one who encouraged him and came up with a new plan for us to move our business onto our home property to keep it afloat. We were about to go bankrupt. I knew this, for I was also the one with access to the computer with the schedules and the files and the payables and the receivables. We were clearly in the red, and this trial balance was not reconciled.

Now, my domain was to just stay in the cut flower garden I made there by the barn, pulling weeds, making flower bouquets, and watering the seedlings in our greenhouse.

I was losing my heart and strength to go on. It literally physically hurt after pulling mountains of weeds and rolling the wheelbarrow filled with old flowers and weeds, load by load, to the back forty of the property. What meaning and purpose was there now in all the work I did with Kevin?

I ask God, *Lord, why did You curse this ground we walk on with slippery clay mud, rocks, and so many strong-rooted weeds? Why am I going through this back-breaking, mind-bending trial?* For so many years, I tried to be his help and loving support; I went along with all his family's plans. My sandals and feet were muddy, and my nails were dirty, jagged-edged, and broken. I was hurt and worn out and becoming angry and bitter. Was I not right to confront him? Didn't I have good reason to be angry and bitter about this deception and betrayal? Was this not righteous anger?

My weedy, green-stained nails were such a contrast to the other woman's nails. Her nails were always salon primped yet perfectly fake, with shiny polish and inlaid diamonds. I used to have more time to keep my nails beautiful, but now my nails reflected the gardening work I've had to do.

I think back to when I was working in the office

at the front desk, and the other woman came out of the room to schedule her next appointment. I admired her beautiful nails and complimented her on the extravagant, beautiful, and big diamond wedding ring her husband gave her.

She replied in an entitled airy voice, "Yup, keep him working."

I was stunned and without words, wondering how a wife could even joke about such a thing. I knew what it was to work hard alongside a husband. I knew how difficult it was to make money and provide for a family. But now, it was all coming together why this woman was booking in for appointments twice a week (sometimes two times in a day), under a quid pro quo agreement between her husband and my husband. They arranged that her husband would work on our home repairs for free while Kevin worked on his wife for free. The receivables and payables were not reconciled. I felt like I was clueless for not seeing what was happening right behind my back, behind closed doors.

Now, here in my overgrown garden, where I dreamed of so much beauty and wanted to share bouquets with others, I'm devastated with brokenness. I even gave flowers to the other woman, who I thought was my friend too. Now I am overwhelmed with grief, and messy mud, and I feel overworked, worn out, and discarded, rejected like these old flowers I dumped onto the mountain of weeds. My new reality was not only heart-breaking, but it just was not fair. I was not the one who betrayed and hurt him. I only supported him, helped him, and loved him. I hated the thought of divorce. I despised this new position. Why don't I get a say in this matter? I was undone and unbecoming.

I needed a break from gardening, so I made my way up the long six-acre driveway. The only good thing about this hard work was that my body was getting in shape, and for being fifty-five, I was trim and strong.

Once I got up to the house, I made myself a sandwich, cut up an apple, and turned on the TV to watch a YouTube program. Since the COVID lockdown, I found myself alone too much, and since the church doors were also locked down, I found myself reaching for one of the only lifelines to my Christian beliefs. I searched for some words and guidance, and landed on a program from Joyce Meyer. Her lesson was "Confrontation Is Necessary."

Wow, I think. *The Holy Spirit is really leading me and knowing just what I need to hear and understand.*

I take notes from her lesson: "Always confront those

that are controlling and manipulating you! The longer you let that go on, the more the problem goes on. The only person that should be controlling us is the Holy Spirit. You are on the borderline of missing your destiny when you let other people control you." She supported her teaching with this Bible verse: "We must obey God rather than human beings" Acts 5:29).

"Let me tell you," Joyce continued, "If your only relationship that you are left with is, 'But God,' then you've got the best deal. Don't give up your relationship with God for a bunch of people that probably don't care about you anyway."

"Confront your past and the big elephant in the room that everyone hid and didn't want to deal with and hid under the carpet. Expose it! Help them be free by exposing the problem."

"Sit down with a trusted friend and talk about what you did a long time ago or sit down with someone and confront them about how they hurt you a long time ago. We need safe friends who we can trust in confidence because sometimes we just need to vent. ... We need to learn how to confront people that caused us problems and learn how to have that conversation in a biblical, godly way."

"Don't gossip. Go privately to the one that wronged you and hurt you. If your brother wronged you, go privately and try to restore him instead of ruining his reputation. When you are afraid to confront people, you make the problem worse."

Seriously? I cannot believe how timely this message was for me. I thought about the people who hurt me and who the Holy Spirit wanted me to confront.

> Turn from evil and do good; seek peace
> and pursue it.
> —Psalm 34:14

> The Lord is compassionate and gracious,
> slow to anger, abounding in love.
> —Psalm 103:8

> Anyone who divorces his wife and marries
> another woman commits adultery.
> —Luke 16:18

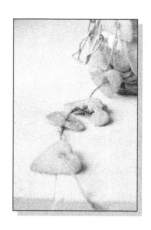

Chapter 31

WHO STOLE THE COOKIES FROM THE COOKIE JAR?

"These were our cookies (metaphorically speaking), and many are missing, and no one else has been in the house but you. We hid these cookies in a very private place so no one else could find them and be tempted by them. We promised each other we were to be the only ones to eat these cookies together. I've been counting our cookies and recording the inventory of our cookies in the jar. There are many cookies missing, and no one else could have taken these cookies but you. Did you take our cookies to share with someone else?" I only asked for the truth.

"Here, you count the cookies," I continued and insisted that he count and reconcile for the lost and stolen cookies.

He starts counting and throwing the cookies all over, crumbling them to pieces. "So now you're the cookie police?" he snapped. "Maybe the Realtors took the cookies?"

"These cookies were hidden. It's COVID, and it's illegal for Realtors to go through our cupboards and steal a homeowner's cookies. Why would Realtors even want to steal our cookies when they have their own cookies?" I reply, thinking this gaslighting has become ridiculously obvious already.

I confronted him and the lie, and I wanted the truth. He wasn't willing to come clean and tell the truth because the other woman's husband was friends with Kevin's father, and he couldn't have his father find out the truth, but now I had the evidence, along with other evidence. I knew the truth. Kevin's anger became rage, and he threw the jar of cookies and advanced angrily towards me.

I went to cover my face, and he grabbed my wrists and started pushing me with my arms above my head. He twisted and strained my left shoulder and pushed me back. Kevin had learned Krav Maga, an Israeli form of martial art, and I think he was using the techniques on me. He lifted his knee and then punched my chest with both fists; I was sent flying, stumbling, and hitting the flower bar countertop. My head would have hit the countertop, but I put up my right arm to take the brunt of the pain. I fell to the ground on my back and tried to crawl away from him as he towered over me. I was in shock, and I got up from the floor and cried, running to the back of the barn.

My throat and tongue were parched and dry with shock, so I took a drink from the water cooler and sat on the cold, hard cement floor and cried. I was so angry that he hurt me that I kicked the rubber garbage can. I wanted to clean up the mess I made, so I proceeded to pick up the garbage can and the broken cookies. I then left him at the barn and walked up the driveway, sobbing all the way to the house.

My body hurt and was bruised. Police were called and statements were taken. Surveillance cameras and guns were removed, and his hands were cuffed. We were undone. We were broken, like the metaphor of the shattered jar of cookies. I was in shock, in pain, angry, and confused, all at the same time as being scared. I wanted my husband back, the one who I thought loved me, and the one I thought I knew. All that remained in this pain and confusion was a complicated mix of grief and sorrow, between a world of love and hate. My world was shaken by the storm clouds of love and hate, abuse and compassion, and this complex corruption. I searched for God's righteous justice.

Dear Younger Me,

I am so, so sorry. You had no idea that what you thought was the love of your life and the till-death-do-you-part would someday come to this betrayal, rejection, deception, and abuse. Our timeline of history intersects and collides as I sit here alone with you in this tragic ending to what should have been a beautiful relationship. A piece of you did die that day, and you will never be the same. I am so sorry that you will question this mess and try to make sense of the inequity of this thing called love and lust. You will question what a godly man and husband is, and you will try to reconcile this thing called Christianity, this covenant relationship. Yet there is no making sense of evil.

We are merely human. We are tragically broken, and we need a Savior, and that Savior is not your human husband. Your Savior is Jesus. God wants to bring you to a new place where you depend on Him, where you come to a place of being alone with Him. You will cry out to God, and you will hear Him answer and guide you to a new place where you will let go of everything and hold onto Jesus as your Savior. Every letter and word of God will practically come to life in the well-oiled wheel of the Holy Spirit, and you will soon be in a new place.

You will be undone but not broken, you will be burnt but not singed, you will be hard-pressed but not crushed. You will be something new, and when you come to the other side of this betrayal, abuse, and pain, you will find new meaning. You will find a peace that passes all understanding, a joy in your mourning, and a hope that only comes through knowing that God has got you in the safety of His hand. God is taking you out of your present circumstance and relationship to protect you. You will manage, you will get through this, and you will be whole again. Soon you will understand a deeper love and what real love is.

There are those who hate the one who upholds justice in court and detest the one who tells the truth.

—Amos 5:10

These are the things you are to do: Speak the truth to each other, and render true and sound judgment in your courts.

—Zechariah 8:16

So I will cast her on a bed of suffering, and I will make those who commit adultery with her suffer intensely, unless they repent of her ways.

—Revelation 2:22

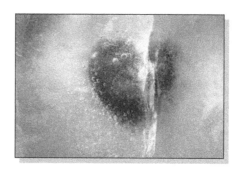

Chapter 32

THE ENTANGLED HEART AND MIND: FEBRUARY 2023

It's still the frigid season of February, where it feels like my heart lay numb and stopped in the deep hollows of ice. Our hearts no longer beat with love for each other but are frozen with the cold, hard facts of pain, abuse, and betrayal. How can I still forgive and love someone who has once again broken my heart and physically hurt me so deeply? How has my disappointment in him affected me so greatly? I struggle with the complexities of sorting out my feelings for the man I loved who's hurt me so deeply, the man I thought he was.

My ideal marriage and husband are gone. It doesn't make sense that I must let go of the one I love since he is still alive and breathing, so I ask God to not let him go. I pray that God would find my lost sheep that has wandered off. I cannot figure out if God wanted him gone for my own protection, if my husband was a wolf in sheep's clothing, or if he's just a lost sheep that wandered off. Do I pray for my husband to be found, or do I let him go because he was dangerous for me and the well-being of my soul?

The decision to hang onto the anger and bitterness from betrayal and mistrust versus letting go, moving on, forgiving, and trusting that God will provide a new way, is very confusing. I will trust the Lord to deliver me from this perplexing oppression and stronghold. I choose to have faith and hope my heavenly Father will love me, heal me, hold me, and be my protector and provider. When lies and deceit become exposed in the people you trusted and regarded as good, you start to lose faith and trust in them and humanity. I must trust my instincts and pray for wisdom and discernment because I know my hope and provision are in the Lord and not in other people.

Today, mid-February 2023, I look to God's Word

for His guidance and encouragement and turn on Sid Roth's *It's Supernatural*. His guest speaker, Robert Hotchkin, has this powerfully prophetic warning for me. He concludes the program with, "In this season of warfare, to stay on track and be effective for the Kingdom, we must learn how to process loss without seeing it as defeat.

"At the cross, Mary lost her son, Jesus, and she lost seeing him every single day. The disciples lost their understanding of what was going on, so much so that they either ran away or fell away. But there was no defeat at the cross. It was the greatest victory that has ever been seen. We will have loss in this season of warfare, but we must not deny it or ignore it because that will build up into bitterness and apathy. The enemy wants us to see loss as defeat, so we pull away from God, we stop believing, we stop praying, we stop decreeing and we stop declaring, but the enemy is terrified at what the body of Jesus is about to do on the earth."

This powerful truth is a reminder that I must be courageous and stand strong in hope and faith while I'm going through these refining fires and this season of loss and testing trials. I must continue to decree and declare the truth from God's Word, for He knows the heart of His children, and He hears the prayers of a faithful and contrite heart. I know that without a doubt, this is God's promise and my continued declaration, that if we repent and turn from our evil ways, and we remain faithful and hopeful in Christ and His promises, we will also be victorious in overcoming these trials. I do decree, that when we trust in God's Word, we will share in His eternal glory, and even if mere men should fail us, reject us, and betray us, Jesus promises He will always love us, and He will never let us go.

Today, I still try to wrap my mind around the fact that my husband and best friend is gone, my job and our work together is gone, my acreage home and property is gone, my cut flower garden and dreams are gone, my children and grandchildren all live very far away, and basically my life as I knew it is now so very far away and gone. I am separated from my husband and my children as I walk alone through the day in this painful time of loss, abandonment, betrayal, and rejection.

Although I am by myself, I look to the Lord to be the very breath that I breathe. I trust God to carry me through this difficult time. I lean into God, I depend on Him, on Jesus, to be my strength, my provider, and my deliverer. I am so grateful to be able to listen and hear

Him speak to my heart. I read God's Word out loud, and I declare His truth:

> He said: "Listen, …! This is what the Lord says to you: 'Do not be afraid or discouraged because of this vast army. For the battle is not yours, but God's.'"
>
> —2 Chronicles 20:15

> Trust in the Lord with all your heart and lean not on your own understanding; in all your ways submit to him, and he will make your paths straight.
>
> —Proverbs 3:5–6

> Turn from evil and do good; seek peace and pursue it.
>
> —Psalm 34:14

Chapter 33

THE GRATEFUL PAUSE

Thank God for coffee. I lift my cup off the napkin that has the word "Gratitude" on it. It's still the cold winter, and I welcome the warmth of this hot cup of goodness while I breathe in and exhale the beautiful aroma of java bean. There is still so much good, and God is my soul comforter. I pause and decide to write out everything I am grateful for on the napkin that is stained with a coffee ring. I write out my thankful and heartfelt note of what I am blessed with. I joyfully fill every square inch of the napkin with haphazardly, messy, yet thoughtful words.

This is my declaration of independence and thankfulness:

- God has a good plan and good hope for my future.
- I am forgiven.
- My Savior, Jesus, is with me, so I am not alone.
- I have everlasting life, so I won't fear.
- I am a child of God, and He holds me tight and loves me.
- I have a beautiful family, children, and grandchildren to love.
- I have a sweet and comfy home that is my safe place of peace.
- I have a cozy, warm fireplace on a chilly day.
- I have a swimming pool to share with friends on a hot day.
- I am forgiven, so I will also forgive others.
- I am healthy, strong, and courageous.
- I have friends and family who care and pray for me.
- I have provisions and food in the fridge.
- I have music to listen to and good books to read.
- I have flowers in a vase.
- I can exercise and walk, and I have a car to travel with.

- I have a church to go to and worship freely.
- I have a photo album with memorable pictures.
- I have a sound mind to read and write my memories in journals.
- I have an empathic heart to love and forgive those who hurt me.
- I can exchange bitterness and anxiety for God's joy and peace.
- I have a laptop to research and write.
- I have a voice that can speak truth and hope to others.
- I have ears, eyes, hands, and feet. I can listen, see, work, walk, and help.

I am grateful and thankful to God, for all I have comes from Him.

> Praise the Lord. Give thanks to the Lord,
> for he is good; his love endures forever.
> —Psalm 106:1

Chapter 34

THIS NEW STOP IN QUIET AND HOPE: SPRING, 2022

The remnants of salty tears mixed with mascara sting my eyes. The terrible blue light from the computer strains my eyes and demands an increase in the font from 12 to 16 point. I cry out loud, "Why, God, why? God, Jesus, why? Why have you brought me through all these years just to drop me off at this last stop? How did I get to this station in life? Why did we overcome so much to get to this place of pain and separation?"

I look around my small condo (1,100 square feet) and feel some comfort from the fresh paint the color of an Alaskan husky I put on the walls, as if the choice of my favorite color might make me feel better. Funny thing is, it does comfort me. This calming, light gray-blue color inspires peace and calm, and envelopes me with a sense of my individuality and my freedom of choice.

The home we shared together for the past three years sold three weeks ago, and I moved here. I sorted through a lifetime of memories, furniture, pictures, baby clothes, grad dresses, wedding dresses, and years of accumulated stuff all by myself since there was a no-contact restraining order keeping Kevin from being around me because of the abuse charges. He was not allowed to be where I would be, and the police restrained him from coming up to the house.

I thought back to the last words Kevin said to me, and the contradiction of those words bounced back and forth in my mind. After he attacked me, he yelled, "Now look what you've done; now there's no hope for us getting back together." He was gaslighting me, because he was the one who attacked me after I confronted him for the truth when I had the evidence in my hands.

Then he apologized after the attack; he came into

the house and knocked on the bedroom door, where I was alone and crying. I was afraid of him. He wanted me to open the locked door.

He crossed his arms and said with a stern look on his face, "I'm so, so sorry. I know that I was way too hard on you, and that was way over the top. I am so sorry. You can call the police if you want; you have the right to press charges."

It was bizarre that he apologized and confessed, and even though I didn't call the police, unknowingly to me, the family called the police. Just then he heard my cell phone ring; he got mad at me and asked who was calling on my cell. "Did you tell family about what happened?" he asked.

I was confused by Kevin's reaction, when after his apology and confession, he said I had a right to call the police and press charges, then he scared me again when he got mad at me for talking to family and when police called my cell phone. I wondered, so which was it? "I'm sorry and you have the right to press charges," or "What did you say? Who did you call? Why did you call the police?" Whether he was just calling my bluff in hopes I would forgive him, stay quiet, and sweep it all under the carpet again, or whether he knew he was in the wrong to attack me and he should be accountable for his actions, I don't know.

It didn't matter anymore. It was out of my hands, and it was much too late. The police were called, and they stepped in and assessed the situation. I didn't want to press charges, but the police press charges in domestic violence cases. Now, since there was a restraining order, I must pack up our home and move by myself.

I sorted through our love letters and cards, and decided whether I should keep this special thing or donate it. I considered the statue we bought in Cuba. It was a heavy statue of a poor boy holding an empty bowl and apple; how did we ever pack that into our suitcase, anyway? We called him Samuel for the boy we never had. I left behind the plaster statue of a baby holding a little bunny; we got it in 1990, when I was pregnant with Makenna. I'll let him keep that statue. So many things had a lifetime of memories and meaning attached to them. Kevin wasn't around to help me through that process, and my daughters didn't live anywhere close to being able to help me move. This added to the most difficult time in my life, and my heart broke, knowing I had no say in the matter. I didn't want a divorce.

I look around my new, small home and consider

all the pieces of us and the pieces of our past. Family photos lean against the walls as I question whether I should find a space for them displayed in clear sight, or if I should hide the memory of him and tuck them away in a box or a drawer. Everything had a painful trigger attached to it.

The black baby grand piano we bought in the United States remains with me and in my care; it stands where a dining table should be. I call it my piano bar. It's awkward in my small space, but I look forward to every moment my kids come back home to visit and play on that piano. But what is home now? I'm happy that I took the horse picture that hangs above the piano. It reminds me of running free, without reins. I considered taking *When the Dreams Came True*, a painting by Leonid Afremov. I loved that painting of the couple walking down the park path. Kevin bought it for me just over a year ago, but I chose to leave it behind with him, for it was too big for the walls in my smaller place.

Remnants of farmhouse décor and flower vases remind me of my dream flower shop we built but never had the chance to take flight. My gaze stops by the vase holding the last of the pink Angelique tulips from my cut flower garden. The petals are now dropping, and their scent now fading like a misty memory of what could have been. These things that made up our memories, our life, our family, and our home, now, truly mean very little when there is no one here to share them with.

Most days, I still wait in denial. I tell myself this is just a bad dream and there will be a shocking surprise coming soon, just around the corner. I daydream that this condominium is just a vacation respite, for me to get away from the acreage work and other demanding responsibilities. I refuse to accept reality and pretend this is just a momentary pause where I can write and heal while our new, forever home is being built. I take off with this dream of denial and picture Kevin surprising me in our next home, the plan we chose to someday build together.

We still had this dream to build our forever home the way we wanted it. I imagine him placing the plaque saying, "An Old Bear Lives Here with His Honey," strategically on the wall for me to see when I step into our new home. I would look to the family room and see the Afrimov painting, hanging over our baby grand piano, which he would have secretly arranged to deliver from my condo when I was visiting out of town with the kids.

This is my reconciled dream and imagined hope for when my dreams come true. I know I need to accept my reality and squelch my rosy glasses of denial. My faithful and hopeful imagination would be that surprise dream that gets me through each day. Can a girl still believe in dreams, in a surprising "Suddenly" and "But God" interruption out of my dismal circumstance? Could I just stand on God's promises and His good will for marriages? Can I not hold onto this hope and still wait for a miracle, for my prodigal's heart to soften and return home to me?

June 2022

I woke up early this morning and greeted the fresh morning after a night of rain. Once again, the welcoming aroma of my coffee exhilarates me to embrace this fresh new day. How is it that I am not sharing this beautiful moment with the ones I love? When will I be at peace with my brave new world of being alone?

I look out at the surrounding buildings and balconies of my new home at the condo village estates. The chartreuse leaves are hanging lush on the trees as the fresh spring rain still drips onto the colorful iris blooms. The swimming pool glistens a welcoming aqua shade that reminds me of being on a romantic tropical vacation with my loved ones, yet they are not here. It's peaceful and quiet, for no one is awake and out on their balcony decks yet. I am alone, but somehow not lonely in the stillness.

I am the only one capturing the beautiful songs of the morning songbirds and doves cooing this morning. No one is here with me. Only my Lord is here to welcome this day and share this morning with me. I embrace this new day as it brings fresh hope, and I thank God that He's tucked me away in His safe pocket of peace and provision. I pray and think of the song by Cat Stevens that I used to sing at church when I was a young girl: "Morning has broken, like the first morning, blackbird has spoken like the first bird." I sip my coffee and notice the notification beep on my cell phone. Should I open it? Should I let social media steal this quiet moment of peace? I ask myself, "Should I?" and answer in the same breath, "Yes, I should."

I wish I was sharing this morning coffee on the deck with my husband. Aloneness is still so foreign and unwelcoming to this girl who was born into a family of seven, and by God's grace, I was blessed with four beautiful children and a beautiful marriage (at least I thought it was). I never experienced being alone and never had to until now. I welcome the company, even if it's through my cell phone and social media.

I opened my social media site's notification content. There's a new post from Lysa Terkeurst. I love this gal; she heads up the Proverbs 31 and Therapy and Theology Ministries. She's been through many relationship trials that I understand, and I admire her open heart and how she cares enough to share her journey and personal story of brokenness with women who need encouragement.

I open her post and I read

> In January, my counselor challenged me to learn to sit in the quiet. And listen.
> I really despised this advice.
> Until ... I saw the value of it.
> Sometimes it's excruciatingly lonely in the quiet. But sometimes "quiet" is the beginning of an anthem song called "resilience."
> God is in the quiet. Lonely is His invitation away from distraction.

After several times of sitting with God in the quiet, I went and stood in front of the mirror.

I will get up.

I will trust God.
I will get healthy.

I will get strong.

I will get prepared.

This isn't an ending.
Every great start begins with a stop.

Don't be freaked out by the stop. Grieve it. Learn from it. Heal from it and then walk on knowing that because of it, what was meant for harm only served to make you more capable … not less.

I think to myself, and I linger in awe of this stop that I wait at. God is surely here with me, showing me the signs along the way, helping me navigate through this new intersection. The Lord will lead me to take the right turn and to know when it's safe to move forward from this stop. He still speaks to me, even through others. He knows the desires of my heart, and He is real enough to meet me for coffee on this beautiful spring morning.

Thank You, God. For You are here with me. I don't have to be lonely when I am by myself, with You. God, You have so much to say when I listen for Your voice in these times of quiet. Thank You for this present in Your presence. Thank You, God, for this stop and this pause.

The Sign with Yellow Wings of Hope

I sit quietly and reflectively on my deck, and I'm startled by something fluttering past the back of my head and onto the cement by the ratan table in front of my feet. What I thought was a golden leaf falling was a tiny, little, yellow bird. The baby bird was an amazing sunshine yellow with little black tips on its wings. It looked like a young goldfinch or a yellow warbler.

I was amazed by this tiny life of cheery happiness that just flew into my presence. The little bird was a bit stunned, for this might have been one of its first flights out of its nest. I reach to pick the little yellow bird up, holding it in the palm of my hand. I am in awe that I can hold this little bird and consider it as a sign from God. God is holding me in His hand. I take a picture of the shaken little bird. It remains in my hand so I can marvel at its wondrous and beautiful creation. I pause and delight in its message to me from above before it takes flight and flies away. I will remember this as my continued sign of hope God gave me a year ago. I had a similar experience where I asked the Lord for a sign.

Last year, in the spring of 2021, Kevin and I were enjoying our morning coffee in the warm water of our shimmering hot tub. It was a beautiful, fresh morning, and we embraced each other's company while we shared our thoughts in a loving yet apprehensive way. The hurt and struggle of lingering betrayal and mistrust was still ever so present and real. I was so thankful that Kevin was still home with me, and it seemed like there was still an inkling of hope for us.

Just before Kevin joined me in the hot tub, I asked God for some sign of hope. Right after that prayer of petition to God, I saw a yellow flutter fly over top of where I was enjoying my coffee. Was that a monarch butterfly, or was that a little yellow bird? It was a little yellow bird, and I thought this little yellow bird was my sign of hope. I wondered if this was His sign of hope for our marriage to be restored.

"God," I prayed, "if this little yellow bird was your sign to me, then could you please confirm this sign and bring that little yellow bird overhead once more to me?"

Kevin got into the hot tub, and I chatted with him and tried to bring back a few memories of our special shared moments from the previous years. I loved these "remember when" conversations.

Just then, two yellow birds fluttered by Kevin and me. I was overwhelmed with the confirmation and display of God's glory and sign of hope. I shared with Kevin how God just gave me the sign of hope for us in the overhead flight of a little yellow bird, and that God just confirmed that sign of hope, just now, with the two little birds flying over us.

Kevin quietly smiled at me.

> "For I know the plans I have for you,"
> declares the Lord, "plans to prosper you
> and not to harm you, plans to give you
> hope and a future."
>
> —Jeremiah 29:11

> Now faith is confidence in what we hope
> for and assurance about what we do
> not see.
>
> —Hebrews 11:1

> May the God of hope fill you with all joy
> and peace as you trust in him, so that you
> may overflow with hope by the power of
> the Holy Spirit.
>
> —Romans 15:13

Chapter 35

DECKING HIS HALLS WITH HER BOUGHS OF HOLLY: DECEMBER 2022

I've tried to remain hopeful, and I've been praying Kevin would finally realize what he did was wrong, and the other woman would be making her own marriage work with her own husband. For the past seven months, I was hoping she was still living with her own husband and caring for her own family. If the other couple was fine, then Kevin might miss what we had together and come back home to God's heart and back to my heart. I still had faith God would answer my prayers of marriage restoration, even though I've been bowing down to

Kevin's requests for legal separation and divorce. We've been living apart for over a year and haven't had a real conversation in over seven months.

Now I don't know how to pray. Do I pray to have peace to let him go, or do I pray God will chase after his heart and then Kevin will finally find me again, there with God? I don't know if indignant tenacity is a good trait or a bad trait of mine. God knows the motivation behind my heart and my prayers, so I pray that my continued request for my husband to come back home to me would be heard. I love what family and marriage stand for, and I love God's plan for the marriage relationship. I am a "stander," but I need the Holy Spirit to continue to guide me in how to pray. Again, I ask God to reveal His truth to me. I pray God's will in Kevin's life and in my life.

I have a new job at a flower shop across the street, and even though it's a bit triggering to work in the flower industry again, it allows me to focus on something other than my hurt and loneliness. The worst triggers are when husbands who cheat on their wives send flowers to women at escort agencies (that's what these hookers want to be called). We know our customers at the flower shop, and when the wife calls wondering why a flower purchase went through on their credit card and the wife didn't get any flowers, the jig is up. To hear the pain and anger from the wife is a trigger that causes an equally passionate fire in my heart. Another trigger that sets my tears flowing is when a dear, old customer comes in to purchase two dozen roses for his bride of sixty years. There are some cherished couples and marriages still in this world.

Last night, I prayed God would reveal some more truth to me in my situation so I would know how to pray. God is good to show me, even if the truth hurts. Today, I'm delivering flowers from one end of town to the other, and it brings me to the road where I can see our old property and the barn, which Kevin is still renting to run his business from. I see her, the other woman, leaving his business at lunch time. She drives right by me but doesn't notice me in the flower delivery vehicle.

I am angry and upset that she is still seeing Kevin and she was going against her husband's wishes to never see Kevin or go to that property ever again. Clearly there is still something going on with Kevin and his affair with the other woman. Does her husband even know she is still sneaking around and seeing Kevin?

Later, I find out her husband does know, and he is devastated that Kevin has destroyed his marriage and his family. The other woman's husband said they were also going through the separation process. After a year of not knowing what was really going on, her husband and I communicated what we each knew, and we each confirmed our worst fears. Both marriages were broken and severed because of the deceptive lure of lust and selfish desires. I had to pray to let go and let God.

Now I ponder what I'm going to do with another lonely night by myself. I ask God what I should do. I'm not going to lie; I was worn out from all my ruminating about what Kevin was doing at that moment and how wrong it was that I wasn't with him to enjoy the evening. I wanted to be the one planning a romantic getaway for his birthday, and I wanted to be the one to get our Christmas decorations out to trim our tree. Not that Kevin ever wanted to help me decorate for Christmas. He didn't like all the glitter and clutter that came with decorating the house for Christmas, and he refused to listen to Christmas music until a week before Christmas, but he'd usually came around to sit with me for a while to enjoy a peaceful moment, looking at the glowing lights of the decorated tree.

My stomach sickened at the thought of another woman trimming our tree for Christmas. The tree I left with him was the one I bought for us two years ago to enjoy when we celebrated Christmas together with our kids and our grandkids. Now, in my condo, I had no room to store all our family heirlooms and decorations. Now, instead of being with me, Kevin was with her and her little children decorating my, our, tree with her ornaments. I also just found out she and Kevin were traveling to an exotic place for Kevin's birthday in a week from now.

I will be honest; I am so devastated, hurt, and angry, and I do not know what to do with this calamity of emotions. How do I make sense of any of this mess, and could God still make something beautiful out of the painful past I've experienced? Could I still find meaning and purpose in any of the destruction that swept through our marriage and family?

I ask God, "Where do I go from here? What do you want me to do now?" I turn on the television in hopes of finding a good Hallmark Christmas movie to sidetrack me from my pathetic sorrow and grief. Even I'm tired of myself and my feelings, and I really don't think there is anyone who would want to be around me right now, anyway. I am bitter and angry and terribly sad.

Thank goodness for a good Hallmark movie to sweep you away into another story and someone else's life, even if it's just make believe. I flip through all the titles of movies that I could choose. Too many of them made me a bit nauseous right now, because all the weddings and romantic stories just reminded me of my loss and feeling rejected and unloved. I decide to watch *Write before Christmas.*

I stop and think about the title. Really? Could the Holy Spirit be speaking to me in this title? After all, I really did sincerely ask God just a moment ago, "God, what do you want me to do?" Did God just answer my question in prayer and reply, "Write before Christmas."

I've heard a quiet voice inside me, nudging me to write out my story from the journals I've been writing. I sense an urgency in His answer and His call for me to write. I've been running from that call because I struggle with how to make sense of my messy life, written in journals and diaries over the past thirty-five years. Rereading the dreams and memories and words are too painful and triggering.

How on earth could I tell the truth of my story

without causing more harm to the ones I love? I am too angry to write right now. I'm afraid that I will just write through the glasses of anger, pain, and bitterness. How can I write with mercy, grace, and forgiveness when I feel God's calling to bring truth back into alignment with His Word? I don't want to end up causing more division and pain, or causing more anger, shame, and judgment. It's easier to sweep it all under the carpet, like we've always done, like other people and family members have. No one wants to own up to their own junk, and most would rather hide their sin and just claim God's grace is all we need. How about true conviction and repentance of the heart? How about keeping a promise and a vow to redeem and restore relationships and marriages?

If I really hear God nudging my heart to write, then that's what I must do. Yes, I will sort through the writings in the letters and my diaries to answer God's call, but for now, it's just before Christmas, and I need to lose myself in a good Christmas story. I still must see there's a bigger story and reason to this season. With God's help, I will find a way to move past this anger, past the bitterness, the tears, and the pain.

For His anger lasts only a moment, but His favor lasts a lifetime; Weeping may last for the night, but rejoicing comes in the morning.

—Psalm 30:5

Whoever does not love does not know God, because God is love.

—1 John 4:8

Better is open rebuke than hidden love.

—Proverbs 27:4–6

Do not take revenge, my dear friends, but leave room for God's wrath, for it is written: "It is mine to avenge. I will repay," says the Lord.

—Romans 12:19

Chapter 36

FAMILY CHRISTMAS AT THE FARM: DECEMBER 2022–JANUARY 2023

I must step back into life and find some normalcy by embracing my family and helping them. I know I must create some new memories and trust that God has a new plan for my life, with or without my husband. I cannot control Kevin's choices, what boundaries he crosses, the fences he jumps over, or where he runs away. I can only control my emotions and reactions; I can be careful to choose a better path. I must be courageous and stronger than my pain, and I must surround myself with my loved ones. I will help myself by helping them.

Even if I must get lost in the busyness and chaos of family life, grandchildren, and home duties, I need to get out of this town. Sometimes, helping someone else and working can be good therapy and an excellent distraction from the pain of loss. I don't feel at home since my family is gone, so for the next six weeks, my daughter, Everleigh, her husband Jonathan, and their children welcome me and make their home my home. Home is where your heart is, and my heart, although broken and separated from my husband's, is where my children and grandchildren are.

I'm learning to put one foot in front of the other, and I'm becoming more confident to manage life, responsibilities, and traveling. There's a sense of trepidation mixed with excitement and freedom when you're traveling on your own. I've come to realize that traveling, managing finances, and navigating cities and airports is just a matter of planning, researching, reading the signs along the way, and praying to God for provision, safety, and peace of heart. Thank goodness for my girls' welcoming and open arms to pick me up from the airport and for providing a comfortable room and bed while I stay with them. There's always an adventure and fun plans awaiting me when my kids and grandchildren welcome me with open arms.

Everleigh enjoyed a quiet trip, without her three little ones, to pick me up from the SoCal airport. It took a while for me to get my cell phone service to synchronize to my new area, and I was glad I chose a plan that gave me free calling and texts nationwide between Canada and the USA. Now that I was Covid-19 vaccinated, travel by plane internationally was a lot easier and faster than my previous trips. I tried to pack light, but my luggage felt like a ton of bricks. It was packed to the brim with Christmas presents and cold and warm clothing, from sweaters and jackets to swimsuits and shorts.

I packed more clothes for warm weather and was surprised I needed sweaters and coats, since it was quite chilly and very rainy. The California drought was giving way to God's blessings of rain, but the rain was torrential. Later research on Wikipedia stated the "periods of heavy rainfall caused by multiple atmospheric rivers in California between December 31, 2022 and January 25, 2023 resulted in floods that affected parts of Southern California, the California Central Coast, Northern California and Nevada. The flooding resulted in property damage and at least 22 fatalities, making it the deadliest U.S. meteorological event of 2023 to date. From December 26th to January 11th San Francisco got a total precipitation of 13.59 inches (34.5 cm)" and the *Los Angeles Times* said, "San Francisco was drenched with more than 18 inches of rain since Christmas, posting its wettest 22-day period since 1862." Some days, the rainstorms and floods were downright scary, and staying indoors due to the unending gray skies was quite depressing.

A good cure for depression is to jump in muddy puddles with grandchildren in rain boots and to fill the days with Christmas cheer, farm animals, and unending rounds of kid's crafts. Between the tag-team duties of childcare, laundry, shopping, meals, and cleaning, Everleigh and I squeezed in some fun times: making squishy play dough with the kids, making blanket forts in the family room, playing dress up with princess and dinosaur costumes, and reading unending children's story books. Christmas was just a week away, and there were so many to-do lists to cross off.

Everleigh, now with three little children of her own, between the ages of four and eighteen months old, manages to juggle her art and calligraphy business, the

kids, her husband, her church ministry, and the home
and farm. Some days, I think she manages a zoo, and
we laugh at how similar her days of work and children
were to when I was a young mom. I don't know how
she manages; Jonathan is sometimes away from home
working for a span of eight to ten days. Everleigh
coined the phrase that we often used, "just keep the
tiny humans alive," and that was our motto alongside
trying to celebrate when we completed at least three
tasks in the day. Just mealtimes alone consumed four
to five hours in each day. I'm so proud of Everleigh and
her husband and the sweet family and home they've
created together. Their love and commitment are so
evident, and they make the most of every moment they
have together.

Today, Jonathan is home, and I hear the heartwarming
sound of country music and laughter coming from the
downstairs family room. I must go down to see what
all the fun is about. What a sight to my eyes and joy
to my ears. Everleigh and Jonathan were dancing to
a romantic country song in the middle of the family
room, and their precious eighteen-month-old baby boy,
Xander, was squealing with delight to see his daddy
and mommy dancing and laughing. Xander was joining

in on the fun by emptying his basket of clean diapers and throwing them at his mommy and daddy, as if the diapers were confetti and rice been thrown on a bride and groom on their wedding day. Oh, the joys of family love. I held back tears of joy, thinking, *This is what it's supposed to be like.*

I know Everleigh was happy to have my help, and I was overjoyed to be spending time with my kids and grandkids. I think Jonathan was quite pleased to have me there as well, since it gave them some time for themselves without having to take the kids with them on every errand. It was a good distraction from my grief and pain to help with the cleaning and the babysitting while they got out to the grocery store to do the secret Santa Christmas shopping. There's nothing like the magic and anticipation of children at Christmastime. We went out to get a fresh Christmas tree, wrapped and hid presents, made gingerbread house barns, and cooked up a storm at mealtimes. We were all excited and prepared the home for when Ellie and Brooklyn and her husband, Matthew were going to arrive.

There were beds to make for the visitors, and family traditional meals (ham and sauerkraut) to cook. I was so overjoyed to be able to see three of my four daughters and their families over Christmas. We missed Makenna and her family, and I so wished that Kevin could have been there to take part in our family Christmas traditions, but things are different. Kevin is now focusing on his affair partner and her two little kids instead of his own wife and family. He's not celebrating with his own family; instead, he's making someone else's family a priority. He has hurt me and created division between our family and what we used to have. But never mind that for now. I do not want to think about him and what we used to have, what we lost. I must embrace that God has a good plan for my life. For now, I'm happy to help get ready for Christmas and to make life a little easier on Everleigh.

I took Everleigh and Jonathan's little car and drove down the I-15 to pick up Ellie and attend the Christmas Eve service together. There at that Southern California church, I made a new friend, Michayla. I met her as we were waiting in the bathroom line at church, and I commented to her how I loved the words they wrote on the mirrored wallpaper under the crystal bling chandelier there in the women's washroom. The words read, "Hello Beautiful." I needed to see those words; we both needed to hear those words and be reminded that we were still loved and beautiful.

Our friendship became dear and close, as Michayla and I would talk for hours over lunch. We found out we both were left by husbands who went through a midlife crisis; both our husbands had affairs and left us in a painful lurch. I was lucky, since I had some living money and could buy a small home, but Michayla was left with two teen children, and they lost everything. She had no money, and for a time, she had to live in her car and work two jobs just to survive. God blessed me with my new friend.

As I drove to pick up Ellie, I felt excited to see her for Christmas. I had a one-and-a-half-hour drive, each way; I had four hours until we had to get back home to change for the Christmas Eve service. It was a beautiful, sunny day, and I left the storm clouds of rain behind me. I had my sunglasses on, the Christian radio playing Christmas songs, and the open California highway ahead of me. I enjoyed the incredible views of the ocean on my left and the green grassy hills on my right. I felt the joy, the confidence, and the freedom of driving by myself that day on the California highway.

I was so excited to see Ellie and catch up on all her fun endeavors of being an influencer, a pianist, guitarist, singer songwriter, and music producer. Her talent has opened many doors in the music industry, from London to Los Angeles and even Nashville. She's always so lovingly expressive and genuinely empathetic, but she courageously puts up with no guff. It was Christmas in California with most of my family, and I was overjoyed. God is still good, and the sun still shines through after the rainstorms pass.

Christmas was wonderful, filled with church services celebrating the birthday of our Savior, and sharing and exchanging presents. We ate our traditional family meals, took family photos, walked the historic park trails, and sat on the porch while the grandchildren played with the kittens and puppies. My girls are very patient and loving and always ready with an encouraging word of support, but this year, I decided not to talk about my problems and their father. The girls were tired of hearing about my pain. I knew they wished it wasn't so, but they also knew that a marriage should have trust, love, safety, and commitment.

Christmastime with Ellie and Brooklyn went by too fast, and before I knew it, they had to leave to get back to their own lives, their own work, and their New Year's Eve plans with friends. I still had a couple more weeks to visit with Everleigh and her family, and we planned to meet up with her two sisters again in mid-January. We were going to get together at an Airbnb between LA and San Francisco for one more night to celebrate a combined birthday party for Ellie and Everleigh; Brooklyn was going to drive to meet us there, as well.

We were going to go to Santa Barbara, but the city was evacuated due to floods and landslides after heavy rain. I'm glad the next town wasn't too affected by the rainstorms, and I'll always remember sharing charcuterie food, the explosion of the red wine on Everleigh's white blouse, and the crumbled cork we had to sieve out of the wine. We had a fun evening of laughing and visiting, and the next day, we continued the celebration at the most incredible restaurant in town. Inflation and the skyrocketing prices since COVID, and the Ukraine and Russian war, put a budget pinch on our getaway, but we were so blessed to enjoy a very memorable time and a fantastic dining experience.

After the 2023 New Year's celebration, I offered to babysit my two little grandsons while Everleigh, Jonathan, and their four-year-old daughter, Jillian, went to their friend's wedding. The rain had just stopped, so I decided to take the little boys, Brandon, two years old, and Xandor, eighteen months, out for a walk on the property to play with the dogs and puppy and to see the farm animals.

Once our rain boots were on, the little boys headed straight for the muddy puddles, and the puppy and the big dog followed, but where was the mamma dog? I called for Ruby, the red lab. Where was she? She was always right where her puppy was. Oh, my goodness. There she was, behind the fence on the neighbor's property. I was so worried for Ruby because the neighbors had three big, mean dogs that got in a terrible fight with her last year. Not just did the neighbor dogs bite her, which sent her to the vet for stitches, but one of them also impregnated Ruby with a litter of mutt puppies. They had planned to breed her, but the neighbor dog got to Ruby before they could have that purebred date.

I ran to open the gate, and thank goodness Ruby came back in just in time, before the neighbor dogs came running. How did she even get out of our fenced property? It turns out the flooding rains caused a bit of a mud slide by the fence, and the dogs were able to squeeze underneath to get out of their property. Jonathan and Everleigh later walked the perimeter of the property, making sure all the breached fence barriers were repaired. We could all learn from the real-life necessity of repairing fences and staying within your own property boundaries and applying these principles to our own marriages. Nevertheless, there's never a dull moment on the farm, when you have children, puppies, dogs, cats, pigs, goats, and chickens.

For now, it was good to have Ruby back home and all the animals safe in their fenced pens. Despite the escape, the rains, and muddy puddles, everyone was accounted for and safe. May, the little baby pup, was so excited to have her mamma home, and the two little boys were happy to play with the puppy. What a sweet little puppy May was. We played with her, picked her up, and held her. Then I remembered Everleigh had found fleas in May's fur the other day, so I put the puppy down and told the boys we shouldn't hold her until she got a good flea and shampoo treatment.

Then all chaos broke loose. Lowrey, the black-and-white goat, an athletic buck, jumped the fence, and the puppy noticed. The puppy forgot she was the tiny one of the pack of dogs and ran off, barking and chasing Lowrey, and the boys chased the puppy, and the dogs chased the boys, and I was chasing the line of dogs, boys, puppy, and goat. What an unbridled and chaotic flurry of animals and kids running all over hill and dale. Mud was flailing off boots, puppies were barking, kids were screaming, and the goat was bleating and leaping over the fence that protected the newly seeded grass. The goat then ran up onto the front porch and then back over the fence and around the property. Everyone chased everyone past the chicken coop and over the hill where the goat pen was, and back down to the muddiest part: the pig pen. What a chaotic hoot that was until Lowrey finally jumped back into her own pen.

It was finally time to go inside and clean the mud off the boys and feed them lunch. We laughed about that chaotic yet fun day on the farm; all we could do was laugh and reminisce by singing the "Farmer in the Dell": "The Farmer chased [took] the wife, the wife chased the kids, the kids chased the dog, the dog chased the goat ... Hi-ho, the derry-o! The Farmer in the Dell." That day on the farm, there definitely was a lesson to be learned about the importance of fences and staying within your own boundary lines.

Finally, the lunch dishes were cleaned, and my two little grandsons were fast asleep for their afternoon naps. I also needed a bit of down time. Even though this grandma of fifty-six is still considered healthy and young, I was exhausted, and I already had my nine rounds of workout on the five acres of land filled with breached fences, muddy puddles, and chasing kids and animals around the farm. I went to my room to find some quiet solace and reward myself with some sweet treats from my Christmas stocking bag I kept in the corner of the room. I reached in the bag to satisfy my sweet tooth and went for the Hershey's Symphony bar with caramel crunch pieces. I took a bite and thought about how I loved that chocolate bar; it was my favourite, but I could only get it in the USA. I wish Canada had Symphony bars. I savoured the chocolate and wondered if they had changed the flavor. This Symphony bar had a bit of a woody, orange flavor in the crunch. *That was a bit unusual,* I thought.

Then I felt a little tickle on my arm and noticed the tiniest insect on my sweater. Yuck! I put the chocolate bar on my night table and proceeded to brush the bug off my arm. I wondered if it was a flea from the puppy. I took my sweater off and felt more little, tiny insects. I quickly put my glasses on to see what these insects were and then noticed the chocolate bar on my night table. It was swarming with ants.

"What?" I cried out loud. "Yucky, yuck, yuck! Oh, my word. Gross me out."

I gagged, ran to the bathroom to spit the chocolate out of my mouth, and saw tiny black ants in the chocolate spit.

"Ew! Yuck! Yuck!" I said out loud again as I rinsed my mouth out with water. No wonder the chocolate tasted odd. I guess these sugar ants tasted like orange wood.

My weapon of choice to extinguish the infestation of ants was Windex. If it was the cure-all to zap zits on *My Big Fat Greek Wedding*, then it must be able to extinguish this plethora of pestilence. I sprayed Windex all over the chocolate bar and the night table and the treat bag and everywhere, until they stopped dead in their tracks. Okay, what now? Can I finally have a time-out, spa moment, without the farm animal calamity, torrential rainstorms, and the plague of pestilence? I finally wiped away the dead insects, the kids were still napping, and my life was quiet and back in order. Too bad my Symphony bar was sacrificed. This was all a bit too much, but it seriously is for real.

Forget the former things; do not dwell on the past. See, I am doing a new thing! Now it springs up; do you not perceive it? I am making a way in the wilderness and streams in the wasteland.

—Isaiah 43:18–19

Do not eat any detestable thing.

—Deuteronomy 14:3

This is what the Lord says: As I have brought all this great calamity on this people, so I will give them all the prosperity I have promised them.

—Jeremiah 32:42

Do not move your neighbor's boundary stone set up by your predecessors in the inheritance you receive in the land the Lord your God is giving you to possess.

—Deuteronomy 19:14

Chapter 37

THE COURTROOM OF JUSTICE: WINTER 2023

Yes, you read that right, it's been two years after the initial discovery of betrayal, Kevin's declaration of divorce, his unfair, exclusive claim on our family inheritance, and now, the possible reinstatement of assault and criminal charges. I'm still not on the other side of this dark chasm of pain and grief of feeling unloved, abandoned, and rejected. Life as I knew it is now forever changed. The words were spoken, a love relationship and marriage were severed, and the irreconcilable differences lay stacked in a pile on the courtroom desk, waiting to be judged. There is no turning back. There's only going forward in forgiveness, to heal and find some restitution.

There are consequences to our actions when the law is broken and a crime occurs. Sometimes, we must listen to the authorities and the powers that be when they show up to protect and defend us in the courtroom of justice. The judge will have final say. In Canada, there is the rule of the land, and the Crown government and the Victim Safety Unit may step in to be the voice of the assaulted and the abused, whether emotionally or physically.

There is still a voice that speaks up for the victim, and we should consider all our ways and actions. There is still law and justice in this world, and we face consequences for wrongful actions we choose to do. We can be thankful for peacekeepers and the legal system to bring about justice. Sometimes, it takes a judge and court to bring about change to an abusive person's hardened heart.

It's sad when the legal system must step into the sanctuary of Christendom marriages and families to carry out justice for the sins some so-called Christians continue to commit. It's a sorrowful thing when we, who call ourselves Christians, grieve the Holy Spirit by nonchalantly walking in sin and saying, "It's all good; I'm covered by grace. Her first mistake was to cry out and complain to family and the police. And don't be ridiculous; that was just a little white lie." We continue the blasphemous rhetoric with, "I meant well. Sorry, I was just having fun," and "What they don't know won't hurt them."

No. God is watching and sees everything we do. God is looking for people of moral integrity and a softened, loving heart of repentance. For Christ's sake and the extreme price Jesus paid upon the cross for us, we must recognize sin for what it is, turn from it, and go the other direction.

God does not condemn, Satan condemns, but God does convict the heart, and He's calling us back into His arms. There is a quiet voice of conviction that calls us to repentance and for a complete 180-degree pivot and turning away from our sin and back to God.

In the Bible story of the Prodigal Son, the prodigal didn't stay in the pig pen; he turned around and returned home so he could be restored to the love of his father. Repentance also goes hand in hand with changing your heart and mind, confessing, and making restitution to be restored back to the rightful relationship with God and the ones we love.

We can also know God's plan for redemption when Jesus shows His mercy and forgiveness, like He showed the woman caught in adultery. Her accusers wanted her stoned, but Jesus wanted to restore her to a rightful relationship. Jesus doesn't accuse the repentant heart, and we also should not accuse. The Holy Spirit convicts the heart of those who listen. Jesus is our Savior, and He tells us he wants us to be restored to righteousness through a softened and convicted heart. Jesus also calls us to turn around, change our ways, and "Go back and sin no more."

If we call ourselves Christians and represent the body of Christ, then the Word of God and the Holy Spirit will guide us in all truth, and we should know when we've done wrong. If we don't hear that small voice of conviction, then we should ask ourselves if we are a true believer. Are we really a Christian if we continue to walk in sin?

Fellow Christians, we must recognize the nonbelievers, the atheists, and the agnostics are all watching us, and if they don't see a difference between us and the world, then why would they want to change and be like us? We need to be on our guard and be representatives of Christ. If Christ should return in our next breath, will we be ready, or will we be caught unaware, in sin? We should all be asking ourselves if we are in a true relationship with Jesus or if we've just parked our sorry butts on a comfy pew to hear a good pep talk.

God's will is that we would restore our marriage relationships. Relationships are not always easy, but one thing I know for sure: It's easier to be honest and truthful, repentant, and restorative in relationship and love than to keep walking in the guilt of sin and totally severing the marriage with deceit, hurt, regret, and unforgiveness. There is freedom in truth and forgiveness, and I'm certain that a repentant heart and a bouquet of red roses are less costly than a divorce. Divorce has a heavy cost, and our dear children pay the highest toll.

> Seek good, not evil, that you may live.
> Then the Lord God Almighty will be with
> you, just as you say he is. Hate evil, love
> good; maintain justice in courts. Perhaps
> the Lord God Almighty will have mercy
> on the remnant of Joseph.
>
> —Amos 5:14–15

Now let the fear of the Lord be on you. Judge carefully, for with the Lord our God there is no injustice or partiality or bribery.

—2 Chronicles 19:7

The Lord loves righteousness and justice; the earth is full of his unfailing love.

—Psalm 33:5

This is what the Lord says: "Maintain justice and do what is right, for my salvation is close at hand and my righteousness will soon be revealed."

—Isaiah 56:1

Lord, do not your eyes look for truth? You struck them, but they felt no pain; you crushed them, but they refused correction. They made their faces harder than stone and refused to repent.

—Jeremiah 5:3

It is impossible for those who have once been enlightened, who have tasted the heavenly gift, who have shared in the Holy Spirit, who have tasted the goodness of the word of God and the powers of the coming age and who have fallen away, to be brought back to repentance. To their loss they are crucifying the Son of God all over again and subjecting him to public disgrace.

—Hebrews 6:4–6

If we deliberately keep on sinning after we have received the knowledge of the truth, no sacrifice for sins is left, but only a fearful expectation of judgment and of raging fire that will consume the enemies of God.

—Hebrews 10:26–27

And have you completely forgotten this word of encouragement that addresses you as a father addresses his son? It says, "My son, do not make light of the Lord's discipline, and do not lose heart when he rebukes you, because the Lord disciplines the one he loves, and he chastens everyone he accepts as his son."

—Hebrews 12:5–6

Chapter 38

THE COMPLICATION OF THIS GRIEF

My breath has been taken away, my joy is gone, and part of me feels forever dead with this great loss. This complicated grief is confusing; I am vehemently vexed and stressed from the betrayal, trauma, and abuse I experienced, and yet I am still forgiving and somehow still hopeful in what God can do. I know all things are possible with God, and as you can see from the Bible verses I included in these last chapters, I am really searching the heart of God and His truth in His Word. Some days, I am still bitter about the tremendous betrayal and loss in my life, for I am still alone, yet I am resolved to put one foot in front of the other and try to accomplish, at the very least, three things in my day: eat, sleep and bathe, or seek counsel, clean, and pay a bill.

I still cry out to God, "Dear God, how could this be? Where did my husband go, and can you still make something good come out of this?" But I am certain God is still in this, and He's got me.

I know there's a natural process to grieving from the loss of death or divorce. One day, I'll be experiencing denial, and I can't believe my husband has left me for a way younger woman. The next day, I feel anger towards Kevin, the other woman, and other people for coming between our marriage. Then another day, I'll start bargaining with God, saying, "If only I could ... If only I would've or maybe I should've ... If only they would ..." I ruminate and go over the situation, dissecting it word for word and piece by piece. Then I hit a low and depressed state that overwhelms me with fear, sadness, loneliness, and hopelessness.

The reality is that grief can get complicated when the loss touches so many facets of your life. When you lose the normalcy of your loved one being with you almost every day, eating together, sleeping together, working together, celebrating together, and cooking together, and now knowing he's doing these things with someone else, it can be heartbreaking and overwhelming.

When the one you love physically abuses you and then turns around and lavishes love and protection on someone else, you can become traumatized. When you lose your job, your work, your home, your dreams, your friends, half of your family, holidays and vacations as you knew them, and your children move far away, you can become anxious and distressed.

I know these losses and changes can be overwhelming, and I know if you're going through a loss like this, you need to have a useful resource of help from Christian support groups and counselors; you need to know you are not alone. In times of grief and loss, we need to surround ourselves with supportive and compassionate friends, praying family, biblical truths, and songs of worship and praise. We must reroute the negative and hopeless pathways of our thoughts with encouraging, hopeful, thankful, joyful, and praiseworthy truths to come to a place of peace and acceptance.

We need to declare these truths out loud:

- I am blessed even in my mourning, and God will comfort me.

- The Lord is merciful in my sorrow and grief.
- Although I cry, I will sing and be joyful.
- God is loving and compassionate in my grief.
- I can let go of the past and look forward to a good future.

These losses, whether in death or divorce, can be overwhelming, especially when they come all at once and you have no control over each loved one running away or slipping away, as hard as you try to keep holding on. These tremendous losses can cause us to get stuck in hopelessness, but I know I will press on through this storm, with God by my side. I will get through it, and if you are experiencing a loss and trial like mine, please know you will get through to the other side of this mountain of grief as well. We will get through together, with God.

I know I must accept the fact that my spouse is gone. I know I must let go of Kevin and let God have total control, for His ways are higher and better than mine. I know I must surrender my husband and my marriage, my family and home, my career, and my future to my God and Savior. May the Lord's will be done in my life and in yours, for we know God is our provider, our deliverer, our restorer, our strength, and He encourages us with His promises. I declare and decree His truth and promises over my and your life and our spouses and our marriages. I know God holds us, and He will heal us and provide a way through to complete His good work in me and in you.

I am still vexed and torn between hope for marriage restoration and letting go. Is this all just some big joke or a well-planned, yet cruel inheritance game gone bad? Some days, I wake up hoping this was all a bad dream. My mind wants to refuse this new reality. I've been devoted, I've been hoping and praying, and I've remained committed to the one I love. It's been two whole years since I've been alone and feeling unloved by my husband, but for God by my side.

God, are you testing me? I know God isn't doing this to me, but I trust He is doing this for me. Maybe God can only use me as a vessel once I am totally empty of myself and everyone else I put on a pedestal, like a god, before thee, God. The Lord allows these trials for us to be completely dependent on Him.

All I wanted was to love my husband and enjoy the years we still had ahead of us. I wanted to look forward to retiring and to finally taking those vacations we dreamed of. I wanted to work together with Kevin, to be his help and to spend holidays together with our kids and grandchildren. We were just entering our days where we could harvest the fruits of our labor. But now, that's all been destroyed and stolen. The enemy comes to steal, kill, and destroy. Satan used my husband and this other woman to destroy two marriages, destroy our children's perspective on marriage, and they've destroyed two families.

I still hope and petition to God, I still cry into my pillow at night, and I try to figure it all out to bring meaning and purpose to this pain. Some nights, it felt like I couldn't stop the tears and the pain that was coming out of my gut. I was vehemently vexed. I went from flat-out praying and sobbing on the floor to dancing by myself in the living room while singing worship songs.

Then I would stare into the nothingness, and I'd be still. I'd know that in my stillness, there was God. God whispered my name, and He told me He loved me, and I am not alone. God gave me a hope, and every morning, He'd give me a verse or a song, like "Be Still and Know That I Am God" (Psalm 46:10), "There Will Be Joy in the Morning/Mourning" (Tauren Wells), "Weary

Traveler, Restless Soul, You Were Never Meant to Walk This Road Alone" (Jordan St. Cyr), and two years later, I wake up with this song: "Sin Has Left a Crimson Stain, He Washed It White as Snow" (Elvina M. Hall).

> Blessed are those who mourn, for they will be comforted.
> —Matthew 5:4

> Be merciful to me Lord, for I am in distress; my eyes grow weak with sorrow, my soul and body with grief.
> —Psalm 31:9

> Those who sow with tears will reap with songs of joy.
> —Psalm 126:5

> Though he brings grief, he will show compassion, so great is his unfailing love.
> —Lamentations 3:32

Brothers and sisters, I do not consider myself yet to have taken hold of it. But one thing I do: Forgetting what is behind and straining toward what is ahead, I press

on toward the goal to win the prize for
which God has called me heavenward in
Christ Jesus.

—Philippians 3:13–15

The Lord is my shepherd; I shall not
want. He maketh me to lie down in green
pastures: he leadeth me beside the still
waters. He restoreth my soul: he leadeth
me in the paths of righteousness for his
name's sake. Yea, though I walk through
the valley of the shadow of death, I will fear
no evil: for thou art with me; thy rod and
thy staff they comfort me. Thou preparest
a table before me in the presence of mine
enemies: thou annointest my head with
oil; my cup runneth over. Surely goodness
and mercy shall follow me all the days of
my life: and I will dwell in the house of the
Lord forever.

—Psalm 23 (KJV)

Chapter 39

THERE'S NO CRIME IN CRIMSON: APRIL 2023

In three days, it will be Good Friday, 2023. I've come to a stop at this intersection in this messy life of mine where I sit quietly at the foot of the cross. Now, just before Easter, I consider my past and my future, the painful revelation of truth and disclosures, yet I feel the Lord pressing me to continue to tell my story, the truth, and to warn others. I'm called to help others avoid the trials and consequences the deception of sin and betrayal can bring upon a marriage and family.

Accountability is not about punishment or shame or blame, but rather it is about healing and coming back into alignment, even if it must be through consequences and correction. We should all be responsible for our own actions, and that includes following through with our vows, promises, commitments, and righting a wrong or repairing what we've damaged. There are consequences in this world when we cause harm or continue to lie and betray others. Thank God that He says we will know the truth, and the truth will set us free.

I've wanted to heal and put a Band-Aid on these wounds that have now become infected with the poison of my bitterness. I desire to forgive, yet in my humanity, I reach out to God every day with my inability to completely forgive. The emotions I feel are human, yet in this hate and disdain for lies and deceit, the bitterness has blurred my vision and the lines between the sin and the sinner.

I may have crossed into the enemy's camp where hate is now for the person and not just sin. Evil slips in for the destruction of the soul, and in this same sneaky way of holding us captive to our emotions, Satan comes to steal, kill, and destroy God's children. I've become jaded and mistrusting because the person I trusted and loved hurt me, lied to me, and abandoned me. I've become dismayed, angry, fearful, critical, and bitter.

I know my reaction is only hurting myself, so I must ask for forgiveness and give all my fears, anger, and bitterness to God. I pray, "Forgive me, Lord, I need to change my thinking and walk into a new day and beginning of forgiveness, trust, and peace in you, God. I forgive others who've trespassed against me. Lord God, heal my wounded heart."

It's now a new day, it's morning, and yet I am still mourning my loss, but God gives me courage and breath from my heavenly Father and His Holy Spirit in me. I picture Jesus, beside me this morning, and I picture myself clinging to where the nails puncture His precious hands and feet of peace. He bleeds out His flowing crimson blood on me. Jesus's sinless blood drops onto my hands as His breath whispers a song to my soul and my desire to be fully known and fully loved. I long to meet and truly know my Creator and my Savior, fully and completely. I long to be held and to look into the eyes of Jesus.

I want to overlook the failures of humanity; I don't want this hate and bitterness any longer. I need forgiveness for my sinful ways, and I need to forgive those who have hurt me. Jesus touches my tear-stained face with His scarred hand and says I am His beloved.

He forgives, and He knows my heart. I ask God to take my cold heart and exchange this bitterness and hate for peace and joy and the agape love that could only come from Him.

Jesus puts a new song in my heart and mind every morning, and this morning, I choose to forgive and bless all those who have hurt me. The Holy Spirit comforts me and gives me this song and a new tune in my heart: "Jesus paid it all, all to Him I owe, Sin has left a crimson stain, He washed it white as snow."

I think about every detail I've had to remember and every true statement I had to give to the police when they stepped in as the Crown to reinstate the charges of assault against Kevin. It was my reality, and I couldn't hide it or sweep it under the carpet any longer. I must face and acknowledge that I was assaulted and abused by the man I loved and who I thought loved me as well. I conclude that I want to forgive, and I don't want to press charges, but assault is a criminal act, and justice steps in, so charges are still laid down by the courts. There are consequences to actions. I cannot feel guilty and responsible for what he did. I can only take responsibility for how I choose to respond to my new reality of what he's done to me.

Because of Christ's great mercy and extended forgiveness for us to be reconciled with God the Father, because of Jesus's relentless pursuit for our hearts, He gave himself up as a sacrifice and ransom for our souls. Because of His great mercy and love for us, Jesus whispers to me the verdict and the sentence; even though there may be consequences to our actions on this earth, Jesus still extends His merciful grace and says, if you repent and ask for forgiveness and turn from your sinful ways, then God will forgive us, and then, because of Christ's sacrifice for us on the cross, and His saving blood, the Lord gives me these words: "There's no crime in crimson."

> "Come now, let us settle the matter," says the Lord. "Though your sins are like scarlet, they shall be as white as snow; though they are red as crimson, they shall be like wool."
> —Isaiah 1:18

> Jesus straightened up and asked her, "Woman, where are they? Has no one condemned you?"
> —John 8:10

Do not judge, and you will not be judged.
Do not condemn, and you will not be
condemned. Forgive, and you will be
forgiven.

—Luke 6:37

For if you forgive other people when they
sin against you, your heavenly Father will
also forgive you. But if you do not forgive
others their sins, your Father will not
forgive your sins.

—Matthew 6:14–15

If my people, who are called by my name,
will humble themselves and pray and seek
my face and turn from their wicked ways,
then I will hear from heaven, and I will
forgive their sin and will heal their land.

—2 Chronicles 7:14

Chapter 40

THE REFLECTION IN THE MIRROR

We all need to come face to face with the reflection of the person in the mirror and come clean with who we really are. Who is this person staring back at us?

Do we reflect moral character of promise, honor, and truth? What legacy will we leave to our children and to our children's children for generations to come? Have we become the generation of moral decay where we no longer hear the voice of God in our conscience? Many Christian leaders watch pornography, live in immorality, have adulterous affairs, and file for divorce while sticking to the story that they weren't loved enough by their spouse. Then they claim Jesus's saving and forgiving grace while they are still walking in sin. We must all be careful to put on the full armor of God to stand firm against Satan's deception.

There's a usefulness in the feeling that guilt brings in the conviction of the heart. It follows us to the place where sin and regret have no peace and no rest. Guilt and shame whispers to the will and echoes in the heart, "You know this is not right, and you shouldn't be doing this." Yet, it's the same weight and measurement of blame and accusation that realizes when one finger points at another, there are still three pointing back at ourselves.

So what is sin and good moral judgment, anyway? Humanity is born into a fallen world, and until we are given a measuring stick or a plumb line of moral reason, we can fall prey to sin, chaos, and disorder, where right and wrong, and good and evil, have no boundaries.

When Everleigh was five years old, she taught me a profound lesson that opened my eyes to simplistic truth of a somewhat complex matter. One day after playing soccer behind our back yard, she shouted enthusiastically, "Mom, did you know that when black and white spin really fast, they become gray?"

I understood her reasoning, but I asked how she came to that conclusion.

She replied, "Today, when we were playing soccer in the field, I kicked the ball, and it started spinning so fast that the black and white became gray."

"Simply brilliant," I told Everleigh. "My dear, you are simply brilliant to notice that."

When our life becomes so busy and fast-paced, we can fall prey to the force of sin, and the twisted trajectory that can put a spin on our lives, where the boundary of our good or bad choices and judgment become blurred in gray. We must consider the gray matter very carefully. The two become unclear, gray.

What then do we know about black and white, and light and dark? In exploration of biblical truth, we read in Genesis 1:1–4:

> In the beginning God created the heavens and the earth. Now the earth was formless and empty, darkness was over the surface of the deep, and the Spirit of God was hovering over the waters.
>
> And God said, "Let there be light," and there was light. God saw that the light was

good, and he separated the light from the darkness.

The simplistic conclusion of light and dark is that God spoke the light into existence, and He said that light is good, and we can see a beautiful and profound truth being revealed. Light can be measured as a wave of life-giving energy, and darkness is the absence of light. The black, dark void of nothingness was there first until God brought the life-giving light, and He set a boundary line between the dark and light and called it day and night. We can learn some awesome spiritual truths from the concrete evidence of science, psychology, biblical truths, and the need for boundary lines and a spiritual moral compass.

We all have an internal navigation system that guides us into the light of truth, just like a sundial shows the time of day by casting a shadow and a compass points us to true north and south by a magnetic pull of the earth. We also see a gravitational pull to show what is crooked or straight in the evidence of a carpenter's plumb line. A plumb line can show us whether our bubble is a little left or right of center.

If science and physical nature give us a template of

concrete truth that we can measure and test, then we may conclude that our mind and heart could also have an internal navigation system or internal GPS, like that of the Holy Spirit, to guide us and lead us into all truth. The Holy Spirit is the Christian's internal navigation system that shows us the moral truth of right and wrong based on God's biblical principles and truths.

Can we also conclude that boundaries are good to separate the line of difference between good and evil? Is there not a moral boundary line that we all can dance around when trial and temptation lure us to that precipice, where we can so easily fall? The boundary line becomes evident when it has something to measure itself by, and that measurement is governed by the universal law of nature and the spiritual law of right and wrong, good and evil.

Laws are pressed upon the heart when we acknowledge, accept, and adhere to the facts documented by the legal governance of the land and the law of biblical truth given to Moses by God. The law is set forth through a decree or rule by a governing body, such as the constitutional document of human rights written on paper.

Other laws are set by the governance of God, like the Ten Commandments given to Moses and written on tablets of stone. These laws, in light of the New Testament and sacrifice of Jesus paying our debt of sin, become a law written on the hearts of every believer. These laws become our governing compass through which we can measure and judge a matter.

The law becomes an objective, printed document and something tangible to grasp, to have, and to hold, like a covenant promise and legally binding contract. Thus, morality becomes evident and something to be measured in the light of the governing law of the land, or the biblical law of God. When we have laws and documents by which we rule and govern, then morality and sin have something to be measured by, thus morality of right and wrong become an objective fact. Some still deliberate whether morality is subjective or objective. I've come to my own conclusions.

We all must decide who we give authority to govern over our minds, body, and soul, just as we give governing authority over our cities and nations. It's time to think and pay attention to the evidence and truth of a matter and to choose our path and governance wisely.

When we allow the Holy Spirit to govern and guide us, then sin will convict our heart and lead us to restoration and a right relationship with God and our loved ones.

We must learn how to take responsibility for our own actions, to love and communicate better. The Holy Spirit convicts but does not condemn. Satan condemns.

I love, I forgive, yet when those familiar spirits look back at me in the reflection of my own face in the mirror, I am reminded of my bitterness, anger, and hatred for what the declaration of divorce has done to me. Every day, I am reminded of my own sinful ways of having a critical heart in search of perfection. I must accept that humanity is faulty, and only God is perfect. Every day in my mind and in my heart, I must start all over again, and forgive, and pray, and give it to God, again and again.

I consider the reason for my confused heart and inability to get over it, already. I seek out the truth in the Word of God and deliberate over matters like morality and truth. This is me in my frail and broken humanity, in search of answers, and I know it may take a minute or two longer to heal. I am convinced that this emotional pain from hurt will soon become a memory of fact. Soon, I will make new memories and won't feel the need to ruminate over all the losses from the time when the one I loved pushed me away and left. Soon, there will be fewer triggers, as I create new memories, and the painful memories will just become facts.

As long as we still have breath, we can have hope for a better future. Again, I must let go of Kevin and relinquish the power I've given him. Instead, I must continue to trust God and give Him the power to be my healer, my faithful provider, and my strong protector.

Some moments, I still feel the painful triggers through the flood of memories and the complexities of my emotions, but feelings and emotions come and go, and I know God's love is constant. Some days, I even consider burning all the journals I've written over the past thirty-five years. It's easier to continue to sweep the dirt under the carpet and forget there's still remnants from this broken mess. I need to do some housekeeping, and I urge us all to do some spiritual housekeeping, take a stand, and speak out against the enemy's destructive deception. As the old saying by Peter Marshall goes, "If you don't stand for something, you will fall for anything."

I refuse to not take a stand for truth and what's right. I will always stand for marriage, and I stand for truth, and I stand for the right of a wife to be loved, and I stand for the abused to be protected. I stand for what is righteous, and I will fight a good fight for the purpose that God meant for husband and wife, and the love and protection of our children in faith and family. God hates divorce, and so do I, but God also hates abuse and wants protection for the oppressed. I know that in many cases of marriage complications, we tend to have that same approach to the mistakes on the canvas of our life. We just want to whitewash over the mistakes or just throw it away and start all over again.

We avoid our own mistakes and our own wrong answers, and we hide from the truth of our own failed tests. We keep those failed tests hidden in our pocket, never to be considered again. It's the easy way out to feel defeated and mark our marriage vows with a big ol' X. It makes more sense to consider our mistakes and review where we went wrong and make it right again.

So many more lessons can be learned, and relationships can be restored when we correct our own faults and look into the mirror to see the reflection of who we really are. Are we true to ourselves and our God, and do we reflect moral integrity? I can also see that I have character flaws that need refining and correcting. There's a sense of victory and freedom when we right our wrongs. It's a beautiful feeling to correct that big red 'X' with the correct answer and mark that failure with a 'C' for "Corrected." Christ is the answer to our greatest mistakes and wrongdoings. He's already paid the price for our sins.

Truth, repentance, and forgiveness are very freeing and healing, like a breath of fresh air. Jesus is coming back soon, and He's coming for a church and a Bride without spot or wrinkle. Listen and pay attention; He's knocking at the door of your heart, and you can answer His call. Jesus will never disappoint, and He will never leave you. He has a good future with an everlasting glory waiting for you. The Holy Spirit wants to lead you into all truth; consider opening the door of your heart and let Jesus in.

True Friends and Believers

I've had some real true friends along the way and particularly true friends who continued to listen to my bleeding heart with compassion and grace.

They became pure examples of Jesus to me, as they stopped and listened, and set time aside to talk, to be real and honest. They showed up with empathy and comforted me like Jesus would. I've had trials and gave into temptation as well, so I can also have a greater compassion for others who fall. We all have a mess to be cleaned up.

I couldn't hide from the painful truth any longer, even if it was a bit messy. I've shared those deep truths with my mother, with my sisters and my dear adult daughters (maybe too often), and now with you, my dear friend. I am thankful for your grace and patience with me and my healing process, and I hope in some way, if you are grieving a loss like mine, that you will find comfort in knowing you are not alone through this storm of grief and pain. Jesus, like a true friend, will be with you through the storms of life.

God has sent new friends and old friends along my path to help me through my dark and lonely journey of betrayal, rejection, and loss. I shared; they listened. My vulnerability to be honest allowed them to have the freedom to be genuine with unveiled conversation as well. This is where true intimacy of the mind and heart meet. This is where our Savior, Jesus, wants to meet us, in a true intimate relationship that says, "Yes, I know you." Unashamed love wants to know the heart and mind of who you really are. This is where you meet true love, agape love, the sacrificial, unconditional love of God.

Loneliness is something to contend with if you're used to being busy and having many loved ones living with you. God knows that it's not good for man to be alone, and even though God is always with us, He knows we need our mate. I miss my mate, even though he hurt me so badly; I know that sounds confusing and complicated. It will take time to walk through the acceptance and healing process. I spend most of my days alone with Jesus, but some days, I just want Jesus with skin on.

Ultimately, Jesus will carry our burdens, and there are times when He will carry us, and times when we must carry our own cross and stay strong and remain encouraged in the process. We meet our true friend and savior, Jesus, here on this Via Dela Rosa, and we make the long, painful journey through the dust and up the treacherous hill to Mount Calvary. We come with our pain and our sorrow, our godly sorrow, to this road where few travel, but this is where we will meet our Savior.

My dear friends and my cherished, close family,

Thank you. Thank you for listening and caring. Thank you for the hugs and the prayers and the flowers and the precious messages and cards. Thank you for allowing me to be real and vulnerable with you. Thank you for being there on my path of separation and loss and for also sharing that you've also journeyed through, yet overcome, a similar loss.

You were the man who said hi to me at the Crossroads rest stop. You stopped and said I was beautiful. You were the new friend I met at a new church. You invited me for a walk and lunch and shared your similar story of pain and loss. You were the neighbor and the friend that encouraged me and reminded me that I am loved, and that I will come out to the other side of this mountain of pain. You gave me comforting gifts and hope.

Thank you for always pointing me back to purpose and love, and back to Jesus. Thank you for also dropping your own masks and false façades of perfection. Our stories are all playing out in the heavenlies and written in the stars. God knows the good plan He has for us. We can know, without a doubt, that we have purpose on our journeys and there is joy, strength, hope, and courage to be found when we cling to the truth and promises of God's Word.

I love you, my friends, and my dear family, and I love to hear your words of encouragement along the way. You send the message; you send the song. You extend grace and remind me that we are all just human, and we are all but mere men. Through our trials, I hope we will continue to walk together through our fires and storms of life and that we can still recognize the divine walking right beside us.

A true friend walks beside you on this narrow path. Here on this narrow path, we will meet Jesus and he will reveal himself to us. He will be our true shepherd and our true help as we walk through our trials together with him. When we're too weak, He will carry us. I put my trust in God and not in man. God is our heavenly Father and our provider, and He has a great inheritance waiting for us; an inheritance that is way better than any earthly home.

Jesus is the Way, He's our healer and our deliverer, and He will see us through, give us strength and carry us through until the end. We will be resolute to finish well. Don't give up. Don't lose strength and courage. Don't lose hope and sight of the goal to finish this race well. Don't lose God. Don't lose self. Don't lose faith. Even if it seems like you've lost it all, don't lose hope and love.

Speak up and judge fairly; defend the rights of the poor and needy.

—Proverbs 31:9

Search me, God, and know my heart; test me and know my anxious thoughts.

—Psalm 139:23

Dear friends, let us love one another, for love comes from God. Everyone who loves has been born of God and knows God.

—1 John 4:7

Dear friend, I pray that you may enjoy good health and that all may go well with you, even as your soul is getting along well.

—3 John 1:2

Chapter 41

THE SEVERED HEART: FEBRUARY 2023

Brrinngg ...

Brrinngg ...

And a moment later, I hear another Brrinngg, the sound of a string of text messages coming in. I breathe in the morning air and look at the empty pillow beside me. It's still vacant and void of my husband and my love. But for You, Jesus, I would have no reason to wake up to this morning that we celebrate and call Valentine's. Today, it's the day to celebrate and remember our loved ones and shower them with sweet messages, kisses, cards, chocolates, and romance, and lavish them with love. I'm without the earthly love of my life, but, good morning, Jesus, I love You.

Who could that be blowing up my cell phone at 7:30 a.m. and sending me text messages this morning? I wished and hoped that it might be Kevin and that God answered my prayer for the hope of restoration. The idea of sending a love note message crossed my mind, and I prayed for God to allow me to send Kevin a message that I still love him, and I miss him terribly. It's been exactly two long years since I discovered my husband's lies and betrayal. It's been three hundred and seventy days since he said he wanted a divorce. I've continued to hope, even though everyone said I was a fool for that kind of love; I've continued to pray that he'd remember our love and come home to my heart. I still wait on God and stand for our marriage, even though Kevin ripped my heart open the day after Valentine's, two years ago.

I opened my blurry and sleepy eyes to see the string of messages. They're from my daughters; I thought with excitement, at least I still have my girls to care and send me their love:

Makenna: "Happy Valentine's Day Mom!! We love you very much. Hope you have a nice relaxing day today!"

Everleigh: "Happy Valentine's Mumma and to all my favorite gals!"

Brooklyn: "Happy, happy Valentine's!! Love you Mom and I'm so glad to see you this weekend and that we could spend some time together."

Ellie: "Happy Valentine's to all you guys!! Love you all so much"!

Me: "Hi, good morning, all my girls. It is Valentine's. Thank you all for the sweet morning greeting. 1, 2, 3, 4 hearts. I love you and all our family so much. I hope you all have a beautiful day. I hope you had safe travels back home, Makenna, Brooklyn, and family. It was so nice to spend time with you this weekend as well, even if it was too short. How are you doing, Everleigh and Ellie?"

I hadn't talked to Everleigh and Ellie since I came back from visiting with them in California. Their silence concerns me a bit, as I consider their pain as adult children watching their parents' marriage become a heap of ruin. We'll never be the same again. Celebrations and vacations are done separately and no longer together as a family bonded in love. Currently, we are a family bonded in sorrow and separation. The fact that we are no longer a unified family that we used to call, "Team Livingston," has taken a toll on my children, and our brokenness is felt by all. We each handle the pain and reality of our situation differently. Some of the girls handle this new reality with bold courage and say, "Get over it already, Mom. Dad's moved on; you should too."

The other two girls are a little more encouraging in their sympathetic ways to hold me, cry with me, and listen to my painful stories. All the girls remain resolute and stand in a unified front that declares, "No one should experience that pain of betrayal and abuse." It's so sad that so many people experience so much more pain than I even have. My adult girls have a challenging time understanding, like me, how the father they looked up to could just walk away from a marriage and run after someone else. We all thought we were an example of forgiveness and the joyful outcome through the commitment and promise of love and marriage. Yet all have questioned and have a tough time understanding how I could stay in a relationship that didn't always exemplify love and protection. I thought we were in love and strong enough in the Lord to stand the test of time and overcome the difficult odds of marriage. We all thought we believed in promise and truth.

One would think I would be over it already, but after

being together so many years, it's hard to accept and fathom the pain of this great gap of separation. I long to be those same two people, and the fun-loving family, unified in the bond of love and commitment. Yet, through this pain of separation and division, I remember that I am loved by God, and He is my provider, and I have a loving family and friends, incredible daughters, their loving husbands, and adorable grandbabies. Although I have a difficult time with being alone, I know I must embrace it and see the uninterrupted time of quiet as an opportunity to spend time with the Lord and answer His call and go where He leads me. I am here, and I will be grateful for what I do have. I will be still and know that God is still God. And I have much to hope for and be thankful for.

Brrinngg …

Brrinngg …

Brrinngg …

My stillness is interrupted again by a phone call.

I look; it's a call from my separation lawyer. My heart sinks and plunges into despair, knowing why they are calling. But why now? Why today of all days? Why would they call on Valentine's Day? I froze and refused to answer and let it go to voice mail.

"Hi, this is Brad, from Family Law Group. I want to let you know that your divorce papers and the last documents to go with it are ready for you to sign. Let me know if I can assist you with the signing process or if you'd just rather have us deliver them to you by courier."

My heart tried to be open to some hopeful love when I woke up this morning, but it is now, once again, shattered. I am so angry and astonished that they would call me to sign divorce papers on Valentine's Day.

"I can't! I just can't do this anymore. I am not strong enough for this, God! I don't want a divorce," I cry out to God as I feel my overwhelming pain and depth of this grief. I weep alone, and my heart aches.

I pick up my cell phone to send a text to Kevin. I ask a quick, "Can I please just let him know what he's done to me, God?" In my angered reaction, I don't pause to be still and wait for God's answer. My emotions once again slice through my heart, and any restraint built up from the scar that was beginning to heal the wound is now broken open again. This is the only way I can describe the hurt and pain this has caused me. The struggle and battle for the heart and mind is real. This discomfort is real. The trauma from this drama is invisible yet undeniably real.

The need to be saved from this suffocating and distressing experience causes me to flail about in search of a life preserver. I've always needed Kevin to be there, to be my rescuer and my hero, to save me from drowning. I've always run to him for a Band-Aid, and he was always the air that I'd find refreshing breath in.

I send Kevin a distress signal by text:

"Are you really getting your lawyer to get my lawyer to call me on Valentine's Day to sign divorce papers?! I cannot wrap my mind around your cruelty, and you have broken my heart so terribly! I have been praying to God that you would come back home to my heart and remember our love. You know how much I loved you and loved our Valentine's together. You know you were always my only Valentine. I hope you and Tonya feel the pain you've given to me. I feel like you both have driven over me, backed up, and driven over me again, and left me for dead in the ditch.

I was feeling led by God to send you a heart-felt Valentine's text and then my lawyer called today about the divorce papers. There are no words on this earth to describe my pain right now!"

Two hours went by, and I filled the time with tears.

Then Kevin sent a message back which read, "I honestly had no idea. My lawyer contacted your lawyer in the beginning of December and never heard back from him, so why today they emailed, I have no clue. I'm sorry they chose today of all days."

He is a master of blame-shifting and not owning up to his infidelity or the cause for my hurt, my pain, and the destruction of our marriage. Now it's the lawyer's fault for my pain. He is devoid of feeling and disconnected from any feeling of what true love means. He is still pursuing his own lustful desires and pursuing his own selfish motives. He has totally jumped the median off the straight and narrow path of good choices. What could cause a godly, Christian man, a husband, father, and grandfather, to let go of his love and covenant promise? I had no idea he was leading a double life and going after his own selfish pursuits behind my back. He went from being my everything to turning his back on me and saying he no longer loved me. I am overwhelmed with sorrow and grief from the loss of my husband, my friend, my work partner, and my love.

I long to feel joy and protection, intimacy, and trust again with the one I would call my husband. Is there even anyone out there with morality and integrity anymore? Right now, I don't think so, but there must be. I am afraid to trust and open myself up to the vulnerability of love again.

I am jealous that he is now introducing this other woman to my children. They went on romantic getaway vacations for his birthday, and he sent our children pictures of him surfing the ocean waves with her. He took his illegitimate affair partner to California for her birthday, along with her little children, and they took pictures of them frolicking on the California beaches. He didn't even contact our own youngest daughter when they were in the same city. In the past years, all he did with me was work, and he put off spending time with me and our girls. He promised me birthday adventures in Hawaii and twenty-fifth anniversaries in Italy that never came to be, and now he abandons me and runs off with a younger woman? My heart is crushed.

He trampled on our marriage and severed my love for him. He discarded me and threw away our memories, our time, and our fun adventures. He sold our vacation trailer. He trashed our Christmas gifts and memorable treasures. He destroyed our dreams that we worked so hard for. Now when we could finally see the fruit of our labor, he sold the farm but didn't give up the ghost. He risked all he had on his selfish pursuits, physical pleasures, and earthly lures. That's the only way I can describe the way my Valentine card has unfolded.

> Why did you run off secretly and deceive me?
>
> —Genesis 31:27a

> He heals the broken-hearted and binds up their wounds.
>
> —Psalm 147:3

Chapter 42

LEGACY OF WISDOM, COURAGE, GRACE, HONOR, AND WORTH: FEBRUARY 2023

It's 7:30 a.m., and I open my laptop to continue my Legacy Letter writings. I see the picture of my sweet granddaughter at the age of about sixteen months old. It's a close-up picture of her messy face covered with yogurt and oatmeal. Her eyes are bright and curious; they look straight into my eyes, as if greeting me this morning, and with her sweet, cherubic baby voice, she says, "Hi, Grandma, what are you doing? Can I see, Grandma?"

I would have to answer her and reply, "I'm writing you a letter, sweetie, and I'll let you read it when you're a bit older."

I pause to realize that right now, my little granddaughter, almost three years old, would be waking up with the bustle of my daughter's family preparing to go to school and work and starting their day off. My oldest daughter, Makenna, just two months away from expecting our fifth grandbaby, would be hobbling down the stairs to the kitchen to feed her little toddler, most likely, yogurt with a spoonful of oats. The yogurt and oats would most undoubtedly end up all over her face in a sweet mess, just like this picture on my laptop greets me this morning.

I take a sip of my coffee and consider my written words carefully.

Legacy Letter of Courage and Grace

To My Dear Daughters and Granddaughters,

I read a story from Esther in the Bible about a queen named Vashti. Vashti was considered the most beautiful lady in the land, and she helped her husband King Xerxes in ruling the kingdom called the Persian Empire. Some say that when Vashti was a little girl, she was just a young princess when she was taken away from her dying father and the only family and home she ever knew.

The story in the Bible says Princess Vashti was taken away to the Persian Empire, where she grew up to be the most beautiful lady in the land. When Vashti was a young lady, the King of Persia took her to be his wife and queen.

Some say that Queen Vashti's parents raised her up as a lady of modesty, grace, and purity, but also because of her life's experience of being taken away from her parents in the battle of two lands, she grew up to be a strong, bold, and courageous woman. She was a fitting example to women in her land, and she became a brave queen who also had a very sympathetic heart towards little girls and women who were hurt and controlled by strong, overbearing, cruel, or unwise men.

One day, Vashti's husband, King Xerxes, was having a great banquet feast full of food and cups filled with too much wine. All the great men of the land ate and drank with the king, and they became merry and brazenly drunk. Meanwhile, Queen Vashti was having the ladies of the land gather for a party in the garden court. King Xerxes, in his salacious drunkenness, wanted to show off his beautiful wife and asked her to wear her royal crown in front of all the drunk men of the land, so they could all look on her beauty.

Vashti, wanting to stand as a queen of dignity, was upset by this demeaning and indecent request for her to parade in front of these drunk men. This was not a gracious and honorable thing to do. She was perplexed and indignant by her husband's salacious request; instead, she wanted to be an example of uncompromised dignity to the women she influenced.

Upon the unreasonable request of her husband, Vashti was faced with a dilemma of obeying her king's order or maintaining her own self-respect. Vashti had to count the cost of keeping her dignity intact while also being willing to give up her high stature and position of being the queen. She chose to stand up for the respectful honor and choices of a woman and said, "No!" Vashti refused her husband's disrespectful and indecent proposal to parade her beauty before drunken men and said "No! I will not!"

Some men in leadership might interpret Vashti's response to be disrespectful, dishonoring, and belligerent to their authoritative rule, but I think Queen Vashti did the right thing for the right reason at the right time. I think she, like Queen Esther, was called for such a time as this. If the king had requested an honorable proposal that called upon the queen in a respectful way, without the foolish presence of drunken men, then Vashti may have been disrespectful to her husband and king, but that wasn't the case.

Only God knows the true intent and motive of Queen Vashti, but her actions in the story appear to be respectful and dignified, and she stood up for what she believed. Women should be respected and loved for more than their beauty, which is only skin-deep.

I think that as beautiful women of the word, my dear daughters and granddaughters of the most high King, Jesus, and as we prepare ourselves to be ladies-in-waiting for the greatest King and wedding banquet to come, we have to see why Queen Vashti let go of her high place and position for a good cause: standing up for the rights of a lady to be respected, loved, and revered as a woman of moral character. I also want you to see the ending of this story in the book of Esther in the Bible. When we let go of something we become addicted to, whether it's love of our own beauty and selves, a man, a hero we idolize, a high and lofty position, entitlement, fame, or money, I urge you to consider the complete making of a woman of character, called for a higher position.

My wish and prayer are for you all to become women of noble character who answer God's call to be women who walk in humility and grace. I pray you rise to complete the tag-team fight for the cause to be brave, strong, and courageous women, but also to be patient, loving, and respectful to honorable men walking in the truth of God. Be the best character of Vashti and Esther, who were called to a higher calling of influence and persuasion for men in leadership to stop the oppressive and manipulative control over God's children and women. Be like Queen Esther, who continued the mission to free her people, the Jews, who were still living in bondage under King Xerxes and the Persian Empire at that time.

As ladies-in-waiting, we must open our hearts to listen to God's voice, calling us to live in purity, dignity, and grace. There might be seasons in our life where we are called to be a Vashti who is willing to give it all up and lose it all for the higher calling to be a woman of godly influence. These women truly were influencers. Sometimes, when we give up and let go of our earthly position and possessions, a new door will open to us, one where we will understand that through giving it all up, we will have an eternity to spend in the courts and castles of heaven with the King of Kings.

My children, I pray you will be blessed to be called ladies of moral character and you will lead by example, to be women of influence, of pure choices, courage, and grace. Let your "yes" be "yes," and let your "no" be "no."

Don't let anyone look down on you because you are young, but set an example for the believers in speech, in conduct, in love, in faith and in purity.

—1 Timothy 4:12

Charm is deceptive, and beauty is fleeting; but a woman who fears the Lord is to be praised.

—Proverbs 31:30

Grandma's Parable of Honor and Worth:
Late February 2023

If I were to sit with my grandsons and share all that I've learned about boys becoming men and the generations of fatherly love and truth, what would I have to say? If I could rewrite the message of history and reword the stories through the golden nuggets of truth passed down in a parable, I'd tell the story and share it with you in this way:

This is my parable of honor and worth, where a young grandson was given a car by his grandfather. His grandma said the car was Grandpa's inheritance gift, an heirloom, and a cherished legacy the boy's dad would be honored to pass down to the grandson when he was old enough to receive it. Grandpa always called his car "Good Ol' Netta."

The years went by as the young boy grew older and the family heirloom, Ol' Netta, the long-awaited gift car, was still parked to the side of the driveway, just waiting for the young boy to finally be old enough to learn how to drive it.

Through the passing of time, they forgot about the car and failed to care for it. The rains and snow fell on the old, parked car. The cedar pine needles and sap fell onto the unprotected hood and roof, the wind and hailstorms pelted dents into the paint finish, until it looked old and dilapidated, like an uncherished rust bucket. The boy wasn't sure if he even wanted to drive the car anymore. He said the car was too embarrassing to drive on the road, and he didn't want to be seen driving the old rust bucket. It was simply just too old and out of style. He thought to himself, *What would the young girls think if I came to pick them up in that car?*

When the boy was finally old enough to drive, his father gave him the car on his birthday. The father attached three keys his father, the son's grandfather, gave to him to a gold keychain with a red ribbon tied to it. One key was to start the ignition, one key was to open the trunk and hood, and the other key was for the glove compartment. The father was honored to give the heirloom gift to his son.

The son received the gift and was appreciative, but wondered how he was ever going to fix the old car to even make it driveable, let alone restoring it to make it look good again. He was grateful to his father and wanted to honor his grandfather, so he took the keys and acted happy to receive the gift. With some disappointment, he said, "Thank you, Dad, what a great gift."

The young son opened the creaky door of the car and sat on the ripped upholstered seats and held onto the rusty old steering wheel.

"Does this steering wheel even still turn, Dad?" he asked. "Does this rust bucket even start anymore?"

The young man did not want the old car; he felt sad and disappointed that he waited so long to finally drive Ol' Netta, and now it seemed like a hopeless dream to even think about restoring it.

"Can I sell it, Dad, and get a newer, smaller, and more modern car?" the young man asked.

His father paused and responded, "Son, I think you should really think about that. You should wait and first check everything out about the car. I think if you wait and consider the worth of the car, you might find that you could restore it and turn it into a cherished, valuable, and fun car."

The young man thought about the old car over the next days, and he decided to trade it in. He checked out all the new models of cars. There were some cute red, or white, or black cars that had sweet curvy body lines, and he knew he'd like those newer cars better than the rusty old car, even if it was his grandfather's inheritance gift. His grandpa would understand; he was young once, and he would remember what it was like to be young and wanting something more modern.

The father of the young man said he was free to choose. He could do what he wanted with the car, and he could trade the old car in for a newer, shinier model if he wanted. The father stepped aside and let the young son sign the papers to sell Ol' Netta to a salvage yard. The young man was super excited to get his shiny, new blue car; he couldn't wait to drive his new car home.

A few months later, the father was reading in the newspaper and called his son to look at an article. The headline read "New Owner of a Junk Car Finds a Golden Key."

"New owner discovers a golden key tucked away in the glove box of an old car that he purchased from a junk yard. The owner took the junk car home and started looking over what parts he could salvage. He went over every square inch of the car and opened the glove compartment with a key that had the words, "Ol Netta," etched on it; he opened the glove box and discovered another golden key with a safety deposit box address on it.

The new owner went to the bank where the safety deposit box was and opened the secured box; he discovered an owner's certificate to his junked car along with enough cash to restore the old vehicle. The certificate revealed that the car was a rare 1939 Alfa Romeo 8C 2900B Touring Berlinetta.

The man fixed up the car, restored it to new condition

with everything perfectly restored and beautifully shiny. The car is now valued at over $20 million. The new owner of the car said he'll never sell his sweet Netta. He said that the certificate of ownership will forever stay in their family and be passed down through generations as an inheritance gift. It'll probably even double in value as it's passed down through the family line.

The son who traded in his inheritance gift, because he thought the car was worthless, almost fainted from shock, right on the spot. He gave up a rare gift of great wealth for something cheap and soon to be worthless.

There's a moral in this parable the Lord gave me to write and share with you. There's some valuable golden nuggets and golden keys in the message for a hopeful future. There's a valuable gift in waiting patiently for something and someone we choose to love and honor. If we wait patiently and work hard to protect, and restore, and consider the matter and value of a relationship, we can find a treasure of great wealth and an irreplaceable gift. Passing down an inheritance of a man's morals, integrity, and commitment to wait and keep our promises in marriage comes with a gift of invaluable worth. It may be challenging work to redeem and restore a marriage and relationship, but there's value in restoration and immeasurable blessings that come with the work. Be careful and consider the true value of the gift you may be giving up.

Our God is loving and patient. He came down as His Son, Jesus Christ, because He loves us and finds us worthy of redemption and restoration. He purchased us with the invaluable price of His life and blood at the cross. He considers us valuable and worthy of redemption and restoration, yet our Lord lets us have free will to choose His free gift of salvation.

We men and women who call ourselves Christians after Jesus's heart are a representation of the church and the Bride of Christ. Christ will always love us and never forsake His own, and He's coming back for us very soon. Don't throw away the very valuable gift of our loved ones, and most importantly, Jesus's gift of salvation. He's given us power and authority to be called children of God, and He has the most valuable, yet free, inheritance gift, and the keys to His Kingdom are waiting for each one of us.

To My Dear Husband

God only knows what we've been through and how we loved and how we worked and raised a family together. I recount the days when you were my best friend and the times that you were the best father to our children. The Lord knows the motivation of our heart and why we do what we do to express our love or sometimes don't. He knows why we choose to continue to love and care, or He knows when it's time for His will to supersede our own will to rescue His child out of a malevolent situation. Maybe one day, my love, you will read these words from yesterday to today. Maybe these words will reshape who we will become tomorrow.

If you read these words, I hope you see the deep love I had and still have for you, and that in these letters and journals that I share with you, you would understand that I needed you, not just the collegiate, book-smart husband, and the financial provider, but I also needed you to be the spiritual leader over me and our children. I needed your time and words of affirmation, and for you to be more present and physically near to share, with me as your wife, and us as a family. I needed you to value me as a woman of worth. I needed you to really know me and love me as I wanted to really be known and loved by you. There were times that we deeply hurt each other, but I always loved you and needed you in my life. Why did you give up on us? Why did you abandon and reject me?

I was your lover and friend in fun and adventure, and your help with family, home, and work. At times I failed you, and for those times, I am truly sorry. Please forgive me, and I wish that I could do it all over again, but better, without the hurt, the betrayal, and critical judgment.

I made a promise and a vow to you, and I was committed to you, but there were so many times that you hurt me physically and emotionally. I needed the same devotion from you, and I forgive you for the times that you fell short of the things we hoped for. I cherish and respect you for the times you were there for the girls and for me.

There was still so much beauty, love, and joy in our marriage, and we still had our God that could make something beautiful out of all the mess we created, if you only would have given us the time and effort, and sought higher counsel.

I tried to be a perfect wife and a perfect mother, and I loved loving you and sharing with you and helping you, but I really needed you to know my heart and mind and to respect and love who I was, even in my imperfections. I wanted to respect you and honor you in the same way. You were my hero, and our children's hero, but I know that when we allow the evil ways of Satan to come in between us and our loved ones, we can all be disappointed.

I was jealous when other women came in between us and wanted you to be their hero, and when you gave other women special attention rather than me. I thought we both had the same boundaries in marriage, but clearly those boundary lines needed to be redefined and mutually agreed upon. You hurt me dearly, yet I choose to forgive you and ask you and God to forgive me for my critical, judgmental, and bitter heart. God's working on my heart so that I can let go of you and the pain, and take hold of God's good plan for my blessed and joyous future.

You have free will to leave and choose your path, and I hope you meet up with Jesus, on that path. Maybe one day I will meet you again at another crossroads and intersection of our journey. I long to have more time with you, and I wish our days were not cut short.

I pray for you, and I somehow still love you, Yours always, and with all my heart.

Legacy of Wisdom

What do we do then, when we're in the final chapter of our story and our best life, when the snake enters the garden, and Satan slithers into the family room and whispers his quiet, seductive lure? Will we converse with and embrace that evil, deceptive serpent, only to experience the consequences and death from its poisonous bite or deadly squeeze?

What do we do when life throws us an unexpected and sudden curve ball? How do we handle a sucker punch in the gut that leaves us breathless and writhing in pain on the ground? What do we do when our perfect plans in our perfectly designed world bring trials, temptation, tribulation, hardship, sickness, brokenness, death, and loss? How can we bounce back when our glass bubble bursts and shatters our protected ivory tower, when our normal way of life comes tumbling down?

Sounds dramatic, right? Well, it is dramatic. Yes, experiencing the consequence of deception, rejection, abandonment, and loss can bring pain and chaos, and the result is as dramatic as it sounds. In this, we experience the darkest night of our souls, and a sinister reality of past triggers and traumas can haunt our minds.

We all need to seek wisdom from the highest courts of counsel found in the book of Wisdom in search of truth, purpose, and the meaning of life. King Solomon pondered the perception of truth in the book of Proverbs, and he was known to be the wisest man in history.

Solomon didn't seek out answers to life's big questions by cracking open the fortune cookie to read the ancient Chinese secrets, and he didn't go to mystical mediums of the dark and magic arts to find our futures through a crystal ball. No, Solomon sought counsel from the highest court where the King of Kings resides. He went to God for guidance and direction and understanding.

King Solomon prayed for one simple request; according to 2 Chronicles 1:7, Solomon asked God for wisdom and knowledge so he could better govern God's people. God replied to Solomon's prayer and said, "Ask whatever you want me to give you." Solomon asked God for wisdom, and according to 1 Kings 10:23, "King Solomon was greater in riches and wisdom than all the other kings of the earth."

However, when our human desires, lusts, and greed come in between our good intentions of pleasing God, and our own selfish desires overtake our better judgment, we are faced with the consequences of our actions. We live in a fallen world, and the fact that we are all but mere human beings cries out that we need a Savior. God will bless our pure desires to seek wisdom; however, if our good intentions become distorted, then we see God's consequences.

In 1 Kings 11:1–11, we read,

> King Solomon, *however,* loved many foreign women besides Pharaoh's daughter—Moabites, Ammonites, Edomites,

Sidonians and Hittites. They were from nations about which the LORD had told the Israelites, "You must not intermarry with them, because they will surely turn your hearts after their gods." Nevertheless, Solomon held fast to them in love. He had seven hundred wives of royal birth and three hundred concubines, and his wives led him astray. As Solomon grew old, his wives turned his heart after other gods, and his heart was not fully devoted to the LORD his God, as the heart of David his father had been. He followed Ashtoreth the goddess of the Sidonians, and Molek the detestable god of the Ammonites. So Solomon did evil in the eyes of the LORD; he did not follow the LORD completely, as David his father had done.

On a hill east of Jerusalem, Solomon built a high place for Chemosh the detestable god of Moab, and for Molek the detestable god of the Ammonites. He did the same for all his foreign wives, who burned incense and offered sacrifices to their gods.

The LORD became angry with Solomon because his heart had turned away from the LORD, the God of Israel, who had appeared to him twice. Although he had forbidden Solomon to follow other gods, Solomon did not keep the Lord's command. So the LORD said to Solomon, "Since this is your attitude and you have not kept my covenant and my decrees, which I commanded you, I will most certainly tear the kingdom away from you and give it to one of your subordinates."

What would our marriages, families, churches, cities, and countries look like if the women and men, the husbands and fathers, the church leaders, and government leaders asked for wisdom? With wisdom, we could have a discerning heart guided by the Holy Spirit to obey God and make the best decisions. Our men and leaders have a King's call to lead and guide, and to better understand what they should do with what they know. Women and men, fathers and mothers, pastors and leaders, if we want to lead and if we want the respect and honor from our people we are leading, then we must ask God for wisdom and discernment, and follow Jesus's example and His plumb line and word of truth. We have a good and loving, heavenly Father we can trust and obey.

However, if we turn our hearts away from the Lord, God will judge fairly for our own good, and we may have to suffer the discipline and consequences of our actions. These are not my words of judgment, but they are God's words, and I echo them in my call of warning for us to choose wisely, discipline our minds and hearts, and seek wisdom. Maybe our children could still learn from our poor choices and decide to walk a different path, where wisdom and higher moral standards of integrity bring harmony and peace and blessings to our next generation. We must be led by wisdom and learn to guide our loved ones in truth. We must seek higher counsel if we want to be leaders in our family, in our church, in our community, or in our country.

It all starts in our own home as husbands and wives and parents. We have a higher calling as the leaders and heads of families and the church. This is a loud call for men to rise to the warning of the battle in the wilderness. Rise up to this mighty challenge of fighting for your family with the full armor of God. We need to be protected with the helmet of salvation and girded up with the belt of truth, the breastplate of righteousness, the shield of faith, and the sword of the spirit, who will guide in all wisdom and discernment. As Christians, we need to set a higher standard of walking in the shoes of peace and a higher ground of morality, integrity, and grace for the love and protection that first starts in our own marriage and our own family.

It's in this wisdom that we lay the foundation that leads to our greatest inheritance and where we can leave a living legacy, of not only wealth but respect, trust, and honor. We are beckoned to live a life of higher calling, where men and women live in integrity and morality, where men of valor protect and keep their promises to love and protect their wives and their families, where women respect those men of godly truth and character.

> Husbands, love your wives, just as Christ loved the church and gave himself up for her.
>
> —Ephesians 5:25

> Wives, in the same way submit yourselves to your own husbands so that, if any of

them do not believe the word, they may be won over without words by the behavior of their wives when they see the purity and reverence of your lives.

—1 Peter 3:1–3

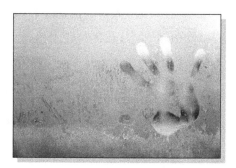

The Fingerprints We Leave Behind in Time

To the husbands and the wives, to the parents of our children,

Do we stop to realize what a privilege and honor it is to be the head of the house, under God's authority, and to be called to love, protect, and lead our spouse and children? Life isn't just about work and the pursuit of knowledge or a higher stature or a bigger home.

The family needs a provider, but also, they need you to be present and to set time aside from all the other calls of duty from outside the home to help, lead, love, be an example, and spend time with your own family. Husband and Dad, you are the hero to your wife and your children. Don't sacrifice your own loved ones by trying to be everyone else's provider and hero. God has set you apart to lead your own family in truth, love, and integrity. What an outstanding call of duty and a position of honor as the head of your own family.

Husband and father, this family tree you are part of needs to be watered and fed with sunshine to grow strong and to be stable. Make time for God and your loved ones and set aside the busyness and personal pursuits for but a moment to have fun with the wife and children God gave you. Love them and share with them and even be vulnerable enough to let them know your heart and who you really are beneath the surface.

When you get up in the morning and are given another day, ask yourself if you've stopped to spend time with God, to ask for wisdom, and to lead your family in truth and love. Consider the reason for your beautiful wife and children God has given you. Life, love, and family can leave a mess of toys on the floor, remnants of mealtime on the table, piles of laundry stacked on the stairs, and fingerprints on the windows, but there is something beautiful and valuable remaining when we continue to choose grace and love.

One day, if only then, when we stop to read and consider these letters that I write, or if it takes until the end when we begin again on the other side, will we notice the importance of the fingerprints our children and grandbabies leave behind? Maybe then, we will understand why we didn't want to clean that sliding door over the last year. There was a tiny smudge we wanted to remain. It's a remnant of the tiny hand that touched it months before. It's the fingerprint that our child or our grandchild left behind on the sliding glass door, and it remains to leave an imprint on our heart, forever in time.

Will we then stop to truly realize and understand the reason for that handprint and what it means and represents? Will we now have eyes to see past this beautiful mess?

Breathe in, pause, and exhale, long enough to allow your mind to linger and look past the mess, to see the inner beauty and worth of the people who have left behind their fingerprints on the walls, their footprints in the sand, and their imprints on your heart. What imprint and impression have you left on your loved one's hearts?

Take that picture in your mind of the image they impress upon your soul before the next wave in this ocean of life washes up on the shore and washes that moment in time away. Take the time to stop and to smell a rose, and to give a rose, and to laugh, and to sing and dance, even if it's in a stolen moment in a messy kitchen, amongst the dirty dishes and pots and greasy pans. Let the children throw the confetti of diapers.

Stop and cherish the time, even for a moment, with the ones you love. Be vulnerable enough to share and show them who you truly are, even if you sit amongst the mess and allow yourself to appear imperfect. We're all imperfect; that's the human condition.

Rediscover why you married your first love and had your beautiful children. Your choice wasn't a mistake or a circumstance to mindlessly walk into. You, dear young wife and mom, you have a beautiful soul, and your husband has a beautiful soul, and both of your characters have come from the complex experiences you've lived through. Have grace and compassion for each other.

You are ever changing, yet God remains the same in

His love for you both, so you should also remain in that same love. Help your husband to rediscover who he is and Whose he is and why God has put you into each other's lives. What makes you both laugh, and what makes you cry? What excites you, and what makes you angry enough to take a stand for something or join a cause?

These moments, these hours, these days, and these years will slip into this present moment of where you'll be tomorrow. Where do you want to be then? Consider your ways and turns at each intersection in life. Plan to continue the adventure with the ones you promised and chose to love, to have and to hold and to grow together. You only have this moment to choose life and love, to be the hero in your family's story.

The schedules, the pursuits, and the desires of the flesh will fade and one day be wiped away like a tear, a smudge, or a footprint in the sand. What fingerprints will you leave in your life, and what impression will you leave on the hearts and minds of those who come behind you? We each have a story. What will you write in the story of your life?

Start children off on the way they should go, and even when they are old they will not turn from it.

—Proverbs 22:6

The fear of the Lord is the beginning of knowledge: but fools despise wisdom and instruction.

—Proverbs 1:7

Chapter 43

RED FLAGS OF HURT, HUNGER, HIDING, AND HEALING WITH THE WHITE FLAG OF SURRENDER

This last week in the early spring of 2023 I, went to a church-sponsored divorce care and recovery group meeting, and a man who had been separated from his wife for about five years said he wished he knew what went wrong and why their marriage had failed. I had great compassion as I listened to him, because I too have asked myself the same question over and over through these past two years. Everyone in the divorce care group has experienced great pain and loss, and almost all have been, hurt, betrayed, rejected, and left by their spouse. A few became so fed up with the petty annoyances and frustrations from miscommunication and disrespect that they plain gave up on their marriage and ran away. Instead of resolving to restore their relationship and communicate reasonably and peaceably, some spouses chose to stop communicating; they gave up and ran away from their spouse.

Listening to some of the stories of marriage breakdowns makes me relive some of my past hurts; these painful triggers can flood my heart and mind with emotions. We're learning and working through the big questions of how we got there, and how to get past the anger and pain, the anxieties, and fears of loss, betrayal, and rejection. It's tough to be truthful and honest and vulnerable in our shared weaknesses, yet it is so good to remember God's provision. He promises He will always be with us, love us, and restore our hearts and futures; God has a very good plan for us all. It's good to have a safe place to relate openly about our faith and hope as we encourage each other, move towards healing, and navigate through this new journey of living single and alone after the grief of loss, separation, and divorce.

I really didn't want to be in that divorce care group; I wanted my marriage restored, but I was forced into no communication and restraining orders. I was abandoned and left by my husband, and whether I liked it or not, his choices and free will forced me into a divorce. Yet, I welcomed any reason to heal, learn, relate to, and process my loss with people who were walking the same path I was.

I hope and pray the effort I've taken in reflecting upon my life's decisions in relationships helps you to also understand how you will survive the painful journey you may be on. Together, we can learn to make wiser decisions with a great conviction, for repentance, and a hope for the prodigals in marriages and family relationships to return home. I pray there would be no need for divorce care groups, or divorce lawyers, or family litigation. I pray we could live together where there are no more lies, no more dishonorable secrets, no more abuse, no more harsh words, no more rejection and abandonment. Is there a way where we could live a life with no more court proceedings and judgments to right our wrongs? Can we unite to better our relationships, our marriages, and our families?

I pray for a great revival that starts in the heart of the

individual, the man and the woman, husband and wife, for the good of our children, our families, our places of education, and our churches. I pray for a revival of faith, honesty, and truth that starts from godly headship in families and reaches out from our pulpits to our communities and our nations. I am a great proponent and advocate of love, peace, forgiveness, integrity, and remaining steadfast in promises and vows.

It takes hard work to pursue counselling, and self-reflection to reach honest repentance, forgiveness, and restoration in relationships. God loves and forgives, and He doesn't give up on us, so we should reflect Jesus and do the same for the one we chose in the beginning of our love relationship. Love is a choice, and God is whispering to us, "Return to your first love."

I pray for a new and honorable way that recognizes the right choices and the right paths to love and restoration for the sake of our family and our children and our children's children. Sometimes, the revelation of truth and the light that shines on the lies and deception allow God to do His glorious work of realignment when we daily surrender our will, our egos, and our control over to His better plan and His will for our lives. When we daily surrender our selfish desires and struggles to God,

He will be able to take the steering wheel of our life and marriage, and make something new and beautiful of the mess we created.

God wants us to let go of dangerous relationships and lustful desires and addictions that keep us from His righteousness and His blessings. When we don't give the Lord Jesus the position of control and guidance in our lives, we succumb to our own destructive motives that bring us to a crash and a halt. It's in the wake of our destruction that our relationships come to an urgent stop. It's in this pause and new season of unwanted change that God is calling us each to consider our ways and to reflect on what went so dismally wrong in the past. How can we hope to get it right in the future if we don't consider what went wrong in the first place? We need to stop and carefully consider our choices, our words, our motivations, and our moral values. God can reconstruct our broken-down walls and fortify our boundary lines if we surrender our ways to Him and have a forgiving and willing heart.

Marriage counselling could have helped my marriage, but some spouses are so steeped in sin they would rather not listen to good counsel; they run from God and hide from even their own prayers. Some spouses run away and are so far gone from a godly path that they can no longer hear their conscience and reason. They've blocked and ghosted the still, small voice and conviction of the Holy Spirit.

Whether I liked it, or not, I had no say when Kevin left and pursued an illegitimate relationship with another woman. Some spouses run, like the prodigal, down the dark alleys towards the selfish cliff of destruction that brings about pain, grief, and loss, to not only one family of loved ones, but to many other families as well.

We need to choose to be loving and mature leaders and examples of Christ, for our own spouse and children's sake. Our children are hurting because of our poor choices. Couples should respect the marriage boundary lines; they were set in place for a good reason. Remain steadfast in love to protect and cherish those in your own household. That's how it's supposed to be. Yet all the could'ves and should'ves are things we can't change from the past; we can only recognize them for what they were and try to become better people in the future.

Sometimes, God brings us through temptations and trials to bring about a changed, softened heart of flesh, but it's only when we're listening and watching that we recognize the dangers we should confront face to face. Sometimes, God intervenes to put a stop to harmful relationships, for your good and for your own safety. Recognize the red flags and the fault lines in your relational foundations, and embrace where you are now, to become a better person. Don't sweep your hurt and anger under the carpet of shame, but stop to consider your past and allow your mind to think back to the red flags that trigger your painful memories and shameful regrets. Learn from your emotional hurts, understand your physical hungers, and ask yourself why you are running and hiding. Learn from them and grow from them and embrace a new you because you've stopped to take the time to consider and reflect.

So where did we go wrong? How can my words here help you to choose better and experience a fun-loving, respectful, adventurous, and rewarding marriage? Well, let me think back and consider this question of where we can make the wrong decisions and where we might have gone wrong. Did we choose wisely when we looked for a godly spouse and fell in love? Were they true Christians and did they emulate and live out their faith with promise, protection, and moral integrity? Are there red flags and warnings that God gave us that we should have paid attention to? What are some of these specific red flags that warn us that we need a correction, and alert us to close a few open doors that welcome the enemy into our lives? Maybe we shouldn't be in relationship with someone who refuses to walk in truth, love, and promise. Maybe we should bring these red flags up in premarriage counselling.

Today, in the spring of 2023, I pray to God and seek His counsel and direction. I pray that through His leading and the Holy Spirit speaking to my heart and mind, I will have eyes to see and ears to hear; I listen and watch and ask for wisdom and discernment before I write on and dig deep into where I missed the red flags that hurt me and where I should've put a boundary stop and said, "No."

I consider Kevin and my relationship; what were we starved for? I ask God to reveal the things we were hiding from. I ask God to help me through the seriously painful assignment of remembering the things that hurt us, the areas of lack and hunger, and the reasons we ran and hid. Where do good intentions slip into evil, selfish, deceptive desires?

I ask Dr. Jesus to help me identify the infection and disease from the unprocessed and unhealed deep wounds and dark places of the soul. Jesus wants us to recognize the evil that comes in to steal, kill, and destroy.

He wants us to shine our light on the truth and to rebuke and eradicate the evil we allowed to creep into our lives. This evil distorts love and truth. There is a battle that rages for our lives, our minds, our souls, and our relationships. Let's have the strength and courage in Christ to shine our light on those dark places. I pause to pray and seek God's leading.

I turn on the TV and watch the Christian Broadcast Network; the topic is "The Perversion of Truth," with the Fox News guest contributor, Raymond Arroyo, who just wrote a new children's book called *The Unexpected Light of Thomas Alva Edison*. I sense a leading and God's truth in what I chose to watch, and I quote Raymond Arroyo as he speaks:

> Jesus reminds us of the heavy cost of embodying the truth, representing the truth, and broadcasting the truth. It's not always welcome, but it's your job, it's your task, all of us as human beings. It's what we're called to do, and the more we are

willing to do that and risk our name and our reputation, and our standing to do so, the better society will be. Certainly, the better our families will be. Only by looking back, can you see the mistakes of the past and what to avoid, and the glories of the past and what to emulate.

You cannot make up the clear direction God gives you when you seek His higher counsel. So, I continue to shine my light and expose the dark hidden truths of the past I failed to recognize. I make a list of the specific red flags that should've warned me to walk away.

I received some counsel from Livesavingdivorce. com by gbaskerville: "Perhaps there weren't any warning signs or 🚩 red flags.

Some people are just incredibly good at hiding their bad character traits. They fool everyone, even the pastors, parents, and counselors. Often abuse or betrayal first happens on the honeymoon, or during pregnancy, or during an illness, or some other time that the abused or betrayed spouse is vulnerable.

"Perhaps there were minor warning signs. There may have been small things that bothered you, but they were brushed off as typical immaturity, and you

362 *Stephanie Livingston*

never thought the problems could ever grow to this level. Sometimes they take on an ominous shadow immediately after commitment (engagement or wedding or first child). Sometimes they are latent and don't emerge until years later when the stress of life and disappointments crop up. Then we were told by others they were normal difficulties in marriage. We were told that we must try harder, pray more, and be more agreeable."

There are danger signs, and sometimes we reinterpret these signs into good, safe, and pleasant traits when we want that ideal, loving, hopeful marriage. Good people want to be loving and want to leave room for growth and forgiveness. Some traits can be seen as positive, until distortion and extreme behavior sets in to consume any goodness intended. Nevertheless, we must assess our own character flaws before we even consider how we overlooked those abusive, emotional, or physical red flags in others.

There definitely were some 🚩 red flags I failed to notice. I received some good counsel from lifesavingdivorce.com, and with inclusion of my own examples, I took note of how each of our good intentions and character traits became hurtful. I discovered how sin, lustful desires, and physical hunger can cause us to hide from our own sin and shameful acts. Sometimes good traits become extremely distorted and harmful to your relationship, and the two of you began to walk in the enemy's camp:

🏴 When your desire for protection, devotion, loyal care, and concern turns into extreme possessiveness and jealousy.

🏴 When your desire for a spotless self-image becomes a cover-up of the imperfections or wearing a mask to deflect your own blemishes of betrayal.

🏴 When self-confidence and assuredness turn into arrogance and conceit.

🏴 When persistence and good qualities of steadfast strength become stubborn, dominating, controlling, and abusive.

🏴 When your decisive ability to make choices and decisions becomes nonnegotiating and uncompromising.

🚩 When your feelings and emotions become moody and take over your rational ability to make clear and sound decisions.

🚩 When your competitive nature becomes abusive and quarrelsome.

🚩 When your analytical and concerned mind becomes suspicious and critical.

🚩 When your steadfastness and persistence become compulsive.

🚩 When your stoic, calm, and quiet nature becomes nondemonstrative, with the silent treatment or stonewalling.

🚩 When your fun-loving, easily excitable character turns into thrill-seeking, foolishness, and irresponsibility.

🚩 When your good motivations turn into selfish instigation.

🚩 When your inquisitive mind and need for understanding become nosy and intrusive.

🏴 When your creative and tenacious traits become manipulative and controlling.

🏴 When your open, authentic honesty becomes rude, insulting, and inconsiderate.

🏴 When your free spirit becomes impulsive and lacking self-control.

🏴 When your desire for love and pleasure becomes self-seeking, self-gratifying, addictive, lustful, pornographic, or sexually offensive.

🏴 When your passion becomes emotionally charged and your outbursts become uncontrolled and fueled by anger and rage.

🏴 When your need to think out of the box and your pursuit for new opportunities becomes covert, subversive, and secretive.

🏴 When you want others to see the best in yourself, so when you've done something wrong, instead of being honest and truthful, you hide your guilt and cover your shame with more lies and deceit.

🚩 When a secret, a concealed truth, or a little white lie becomes a mountainous, giant heap of lies.

🚩 When you set out to be an inclusive, friendly team builder and when things aren't going your way, you start to conspire and coerce, and triangulate others into teaming up against the person you want to control and punish for your own selfish gain or to continue the cover-up of the lie.

🚩 When your desire for financial gain, freedom, and concern for family provision and investment becomes menacing, intimidating, and entitled, motivated by power, selfish gain, status, financial abuse, manipulation, and control.

🚩 When your desire for perfection and righteousness in your own self turns into a hypocritical need for others to be perfect and righteous as well. When you become hypocritical and haven't been able to turn from your own sin, and when you've failed to take the plank out of your own eye before pointing to the speck in someone else's eye.

🚩 When you embrace freedom of choice and want to build a new future, but you become careless and inconsiderate to your promises and abandon, desert, and reject the ones you love.

🚩 When your appropriate mix of family life, work, and play becomes imbalanced due to a lack of self-control and not setting boundaries and limits. When the need to relax and have fun turns into thrill-seeking and extreme need to self-medicate through addictive means of pain numbing, alcohol, drugs, pornography, gambling, or risky sexual behaviors.

🚩 When your desire to please others becomes a failure to be true to yourself and ségfutó.

your God. When people pleasing becomes more important than God pleasing.

🏴When your relaxed and carefree attitude unintentionally becomes forgetful, inconsiderate, careless, disrespectful, disregarding communication of crucial details.

🏴 When your polite excuses of not being fussy or not wanting to make a big deal becomes neglecting and forgetting important birthdays and anniversaries with your own spouse and children.

🏴 When your desire to be peaceful becomes avoidance of confrontation and disagreement. Instead of facing an important discussion and truth, you avoid the topic, cover it up, deflect, gaslight, stonewall, and fail to seek out good counsel.

🏴 When your need for love, acceptance, and approval becomes prideful, selfish, and narcissistic.

🚩 When your insistence turns into anger, rage, abuse, or dangerous and risky behavior.

We've all been guilty of narcissistic behavior and egotistical character traits since we're all born with a sinful nature. These terms have become all too easily used to accuse people and label their character. I don't want to be cavalier in their use, so for a better understanding of the differences between being a narcissist and an egotist, I quote Lesli Doares from wellandgood.com: "Narcissists have a need for constant admiration and will actively seek it out, and they're often shattered by criticism, reacting poorly to it. The egotist believes they're somehow better or more important than everyone else."

Dear Younger Me,

You've taken a pause and recounted your past experiences. You've done the hard work to list the specific memories and 🚩 red flags you failed to notice and didn't heed their warnings. Your list started from the dating process to where you are now. It was a triggering, painful list that consumed three entire pages of memories. You've come out of a painful and abusive relationship, and unless a couple desires to seek God's good will and good counsel, there's little hope for change and a better relationship. Because of your experience, you will help others through the process of considering the ⚑ red flags and use them as talking points to help others through the healing process. We can't embrace the healing process until we recognize the cause for our painful and triggering symptoms. We're all learning. It's a process we must allow ourselves to go through.

It may sound strange to list all these ⚑ red flags onto a white sheet of paper and yet not recognize them as overlooked warning signals. In the past, you laughed off the warning signals because of how uncomfortable they made you feel, or you had quiet hope for people to become better. You had to see the professional's list and add to your own list of ⚑ red flags to finally see the sin for what it is.

Some of us make seriously wrong choices and then wonder what went wrong. To everyone, and even to myself, Kevin and I appeared to be a lovely

Christian couple, and we wanted our relationship to be all that we idealized and dreamed it to be. In all reality, it wasn't the way we dreamed it would be. It wasn't the way it was supposed to be.

I am thankful God has a better plan and He cares enough to protect us and take us out of a dangerous and unloving relationship. God allowed for divorce to rescue his dear daughters and sons out of abusive relationships and release them from harm. God forgives us when we acknowledge our own sin, and when we repent, He is merciful enough to forgive. God is our source that restores us into right relationships. When we've healed and recovered from the pain and the hurt, and when we've cried all the tears that we have, we can exchange all our regrets and all our 🚩 red flags for a white flag 🏳. We can confidently wave our white flag 🏳 of surrender and peace, and bravely walk into a new day and a new beginning, where God reveals His greater hope and His greater plan, which includes a far superior inheritance than we could ever humanly imagine.

There's a fine balance and a tightrope walk of self-control in love and in peace.

Warning against Adultery

My son, keep your father's command
and do not forsake your mother's teaching.
Bind them always on your heart;
fasten them around your neck.
When you walk, they will guide you;
when you sleep, they will watch over you;
when you awake, they will speak to you.
For this command is a lamp,
this teaching is a light,
and correction and instruction
are the way to life,
keeping you from your neighbor's wife,
from the smooth talk of a wayward woman.
Do not lust in your heart after her beauty
or let her captivate you with her eyes.
For a prostitute can be had for a loaf of bread,
but another man's wife preys on your very
life.
Can a man scoop fire into his lap
without his clothes being burned?
Can a man walk on hot coals
without his feet being scorched?

So is he who sleeps with another man's wife;
no one who touches her will go unpunished.
People do not despise a thief if he steals
to satisfy his hunger when he is starving.
Yet if he is caught, he must pay sevenfold,
though it costs him all the wealth of his house.
But a man who commits adultery has no
sense;
whoever does so destroys himself.
Blows and disgrace are his lot,
and his shame will never be wiped away.

—Proverbs 6:20–33

For of this you can be sure: No immoral,
impure or greedy person—such a person
is an idolater—has any inheritance in the
kingdom of Christ and of God.

—Ephesians 5:5

The best morality in the world will not
prove a man to be a Christian, but if a man
has not morality, it proves that he is not a
child of God.

—C. H. Spurgeon

Where there is no "moral gravity"—that is, no force that draws us to the center—there is spiritual weightlessness. We float on feelings that will carry us where we never meant to go; we bubble with emotional experiences that we often take for spiritual ones; and we are puffed up with pride. Instead of seriousness, there is foolishness. Instead of gravity, flippancy. Sentimentality takes the place of theology. Our reference point will never serve to keep our feet on solid rock, for our reference point, until we answer God's call, is merely ourselves. We cannot possibly tell which end is up. Paul calls them fools who "measure themselves by themselves, to find in themselves their own standard of comparison!"

—Elisabeth Elliot

Chapter 44

A GLIMPSE OF HEAVEN

I could not know that the sunny day Kevin and I drove my dad to the hospital in the spring of May 2017, it would be the last time we would see my dad. I didn't know it was our last drive and our last conversation and our last hug. Dad's health was weakening, and his heart was failing from complications with his diabetes and the imbalance of his insulin and heart medications. He no longer had strength in his legs to support himself. We determined he would get the best care if we brought him to the hospital. He was sick and frail, and we had to support his walk to the vehicle. It was painfully difficult for me, his youngest daughter, to admit that his body was weak and failing. I had to be his strength as he leaned on me to support his weight by lifting him into the front seat of the car. It was heartbreaking to see Dad in that condition since he was always my support and my strength when I was a little girl.

Kevin drove the car carefully to the hospital while Dad was in the front seat (I was in the back). I reached for my dad's hand to hold as we unknowingly took his last car ride. We commented on how the day was sunny and beautiful, and we pointed to the fragrant lilacs and brilliant tulips along the way.

"Dad," I said softly as I held his hand, "I love you so much, and you are the best dad that any daughter could ever ask for."

He squeezed my hand and said he loved me too.

We checked him into his hospital room and showed him some pictures of Everleigh and Jonathan's new puppy and told him we had a flight going out to California the next morning. We already bought our plane tickets to see Everleigh and Brooklyn and their husbands for the Mother's Day weekend. We stayed with Dad for a few hours and then gave him a big, reassuring hug, and said we would see him next week when we returned. All we could do was pray and hope for the best.

We didn't make it back in time; I was the last one to talk to my dad on the phone, long distance, since every other family member was by his side that evening when he left us and was taken up to heaven. When I spoke to him on the phone, I think he could hear me, but he could no longer speak. I sobbed on the phone and said that I loved him so much and we'll be together soon again.

We were in a restaurant parking lot, and I broke down crying as my girls and Kevin supported me with their hugs. I couldn't believe Dad was gone. I would never see him again, this side of heaven. I was his youngest, and I remembered when he danced with me at my wedding. I felt like Cinderella when I danced with my daddy. I loved Dad so much. He was not perfect, but he was a good, loving, and godly man; a good husband; and a wonderful, protective, and providing father.

I was heartbroken and quiet the next day as I comprehended that my dad was gone forever from our lives here. Life and our time here on earth are but a blink when considered through the lens of eternity. We flew back home that Mother's Day weekend, and we were both sad and grieving. I knew Kevin also admired my dad and looked up to him. I quietly prayed as I looked out of the airplane window and asked God, "Lord, could you give me a glimpse of what Dad is seeing in heaven with you today?" I prayed and hoped that God would talk to me.

He did. God said to me in my heart and mind, *Okay, then put on your Son-glasses.*

I thought, *What? That would be weird to put my sunglasses on in an airplane,* but I did. I reached for my glasses that were tucked in the seat pocket in front of me. I looked out of the airplane window and over the wing to the earth down below with my sunglasses on. I couldn't believe what I was seeing as we flew over the Pacific Northwest. I was in glorious amazement.

I could see mountains, and valleys, and streams, and mountaintop lakes clearly below me as we flew overtop. Through the window, with my Son-glasses on, I was drawn to the life-giving water below, in forms of lakes, rivers, and mountaintop streams. Through the lens of my sunglasses, all the waters turned into iridescent, rainbow colors. To my amazement, all the rivers and streams were bright oranges, bright fuchsias, and purples, and blues, chartreuses, and yellows. It was a glorious sight! I was amazed that God showed me this awesome and wonderful thing!

The Holy Spirit whispered in my being that what I was seeing was just a glimpse of heaven and this was just a sample of what Dad was seeing, for that first time, when he stepped into eternity with Jesus. I thought that it was a miracle, and I couldn't understand how I had seen all the living water sources turn into beautiful, iridescent, colors of the rainbow. The vibrant colors of the rainbow serve as a reminder of God's faithfulness and protection, and it symbolizes hope and renewal. Later, I told Kevin what I had seen, and he said it was probably because my glasses were polarized. I didn't know for sure, but I felt it was God showing me a glimpse into His wonderful heavens that await all who believe in Him.

Dad was a good and God-fearing man of integrity. Even though he was human and not perfect, which my mom could attest to, I will always remember his love, his humor, and his desire to teach his kids well and in our heavenly Father's ways.

Today, in April 2023, this is one of my last journal entries before submitting my manuscript for print. I reflect on that day after my dad died, when God gave me a glimpse of heaven and consider what it takes to be a good, godly man, husband, and father, and I ask God what He wants to show me about good men. I thought that Kevin, my husband, was a good man, but he left me, and he hurt me, and he lied to me, and he betrayed me. How can a good and godly man do this? Where does the fine line of fallen humanity and purely evil intention begin?

How could a Christian husband be so consumed by temptation and run to something that's far from God's will? What consumes a man's thoughts, his mind, his heart, and his flesh so intensely that he would hurt, betray, reject, and abandon his wife, who loved him so deeply for the last thirty-five years? I was his helper, his friend, and his lover. These questions consume me; these things I can't understand consume me. Yet I want to feel love and trust, and laugh with a husband who walks by my side again. I want to remain in Christ, but yes, I would love to be in a loving and godly relationship that consumes my heart.

I desire to be consumed in God's will as I cling to Jesus and His unconditional agape love. I long to fully know the phileo love of a friend and embrace the eros love of an intimate husband-and-wife union. It's the introduction of a new calling to the heart and mission for the good passions that move us and make our heart beat once again. I anticipate the new thing God is doing, and although it's not in plain sight yet, it's just around the corner. This is my desire and my hope. This is where I discover my Well Day.

It's now the springtime of 2023, and new life is budding into bloom; the roses and lilies are adorned in their colorful beauty, giving off the fresh, sweet aroma of new life. I anticipate this new thing and the warm sunshine that wants to kiss my cheeks to remind me I am loved, yet I remain alone, for now. I am now officially divorced, although I haven't signed any paperwork. It takes two to form a union, but it only takes one to leave. I must see God's will of protection in this process, and I will continue to wait like the bride awaiting the return of her Bridegroom, Christ. I anticipate Jesus's return is so near, and I look forward to His coming, but as God said in Genesis, "It's not good for man [or woman] to be alone." Refinement has a waiting process, so I wait.

I'm still having coffee with God and read His Word and pray, and wait, alone, as I live and find joy in a newfound purpose. I'm waiting on the justice system and the courts to see if they find Kevin guilty of aggravated assault or simple assault. We are waiting to see if he will be prosecuted by indictment, where the maximum penalty is five years incarceration, or if he is prosecuted by summary conviction, where the penalty is more lenient. The authorities have informed me the court proceedings are to take place in the spring of 2024. I will wait, we will wait, and we will pray for God's will to be done.

The Lord says that vengeance is His, and His justice will prevail. I do continue to pray for Kevin over these next months and for God's will to be done. Whether it's just here on earth, or as it is in heaven, God's justice will prevail, and we will all have to answer for what we've done here on earth at some point in time. On earth, we have a justice system, and Kevin may be faced with the consequences of his abuse and assault.

I long to know, and I have a hopeful and thankful prayer for a godly husband to come into my life, and I ask God to show me there are still good men in this world. I will wait.

I reach for the remote to turn on the Miracle Channel on the television. I see Pastor Leon Fontaine speak. My mom said he recently passed away, but I still see him preach on the TV. I'm not sure if he's still alive; the program may be a rerun, so I seek out the truth if he's gone to heaven or not.

He did, Leon Fontaine did pass away, but his legacy of being a good leader and man of God, as pastor and CEO of the Miracle Channel, still lives on. I click on his celebration of life video on YouTube, and I am full of sorrow that such a wonderful man of God is now passed away onto glory. We can find comfort in knowing he is in a more wonderful home with Jesus in heaven. He was almost sixty years old, and he, just like my own dad, had a beautiful wife, four lovely daughters, a son, and loving in-laws and cherished grandchildren.

Pastor Leon Fontaine's beautiful, broken-hearted wife, Sally, goes on the church platform, supported by her children. She can hardly speak as she is experiencing so much grief and sorrow. She said she could have never imagined that this could happen to them, and she marvelled at how her husband had the wisdom of Solomon. Pastor Fontaine died suddenly and will forever be remembered as a good and humble man who said it was never about him, but it was always about Jesus. Leon's death was sudden; according to the reporting from the *Winnipeg Sun*, he died from an aggressive form of cancer. His wife, his children, and everyone who knew him weren't prepared to say goodbye so soon. Our time is short and our last days here on earth can catch us unaware. Be prepared and ready now, for we will all, sooner or later, meet our maker.

Leon's family had nothing but good and excellent things to say about him. His son, Zach Fontaine, left an impression of his father on everyone's heart as he spoke about how he always made everyone feel loved, valued, and full of hope. He said his father and leader of the church wasn't just a man who "talked the talk," but he was a man who also "walked the walk." He was known to say, "Your kids don't do what you say; they do what you do." When Leon's son-in-law, David, spoke, he said his father-in-law reminded him on his wedding day that as pastors and husbands, "We don't do divorces, we do funerals."

I'm sure there isn't a person who knew Leon Fontaine or heard him speak who wasn't impacted by his life, his ministry, and his legacy that he left behind for us and generations to come. He was a man of promise and love for his wife and family, and he finished well in his calling and fulfillment as a man after God's heart. What a beautiful memory of a man we all could only hope to emulate. I'm sure God welcomed him into His heavenly home and said, "Well done, my good and faithful servant."

Teach us to number our days that we may
gain a heart of wisdom.

—Psalm 90:12

Now faith is confidence in what we hope
for and assurance about what we do
not see.

—Hebrews 11:1

The faith and love that spring from the
hope stored up for you in heaven and
about which you have already heard in
the true message of the gospel.

—Colossians 1:5

Then I saw "a new heaven and a new
earth," for the first heaven and the first
earth had passed away, and there was
no longer any sea. I saw the Holy City,
the new Jerusalem, coming down out of
heaven from God, prepared as a bride
beautifully dressed for her husband."

—Revelation 21:12

His master replied, "Well done, good and faithful servant! You have been faithful with a few things; I will put you in charge of many things. Come and share your master's happiness!"

—Matthew 25:23

Prayer and Letter of Legacy and Trust

Dear God, my heavenly Father,

I stand in awe of You and Your glory. You were the Alpha in the beginning, and You are the Omega in the end. Your love and Your gracious mercy are unending. You said You created me before the foundations of the earth were laid. Lord God, thank You that You designed and created me with a plan and a purpose, and You considered me worth saving through the sacrifice of Your Son, Jesus Christ.

Your Word and Your Spirit were with You in the beginning, and You sent Your Word to become flesh, and His name is Jesus, the Messiah and Savior sent to redeem the world and save us from the sin that ensnares and entangles us to death and condemnation. Jesus,

You are not just my omnipotent Father, but You are my redeemer, my friend, my good counsellor, and my great physician. Lord God, I put my trust in You to be my provider, my help in time of trouble, and that You will restore me and heal my heart, my soul, my mind, and my body.

Lord, forgive us for where we went wrong and for when we chose the wrong path that hurt others. Forgive us for our sins and for betraying You through dishonoring our marriage and for not being a good example to our children. Forgive us for dishonoring You through lies and deceit. Father, God, if You find any favor in me, and anything righteous, because Jesus stands before me, and because I love You, and I love Your Word in which You promise, please forgive me of my trespasses, and use me, and consider me as Your own, Your beloved.

You say, Lord, in John 15:7, "If you remain in me and my words remain in you, ask whatever you wish, and it will be done for you."

God, would You first grant me wisdom and discernment to know Your will for my life and the direction that I should go. Lord, I surrender all of it to You. I surrender my husband, my marriage, my family, my friends, my home, my work, and the desires of my heart to You, God. I lay my Isaak down; the things of this world that I dearly love, maybe all too much. I will lay my marriage down at the altar and the foot of your cross. Lord, I give it up and surrender all to you, my God. Do with my life, and my loved ones, what You will, Lord.

But God, if there is a "suddenly" in Your redemptive story, if there would be a message of a change of heart that comes from Your heavenly address sent from "Out of the Blue," Lord, if it's in Your will, would You please redeem and restore my marriage and would You bring me and my spouse back to Your throne room of mercy, where You will not let us go out of Your hand? If You will leave the ninety-nine to find that one lost sheep, Lord, soften my heart and my spouse's heart, and restore our marriage. Bring us back together to love each other in the same way that Christ loves the church. Lord, would You consider my petition and bring my spouse back home and restore our love into something new? Yet, it's not my will, but Thy will, dear God, and help me to let go of what I shouldn't have. Let me be at peace with Your will and Your direction, my God, and my Lord.

God, Your Word says that You hate divorce. I didn't want a divorce, so Lord, hear my prayer if this is Your will. Restore my broken heart back to love in truth and in purity, with softness of flesh. Lord, I will trust in You and Your Word. I will surrender and submit to Your good will and supreme authority, and if You should bring me my new, godly husband, I will love him and respect him as a man and a father of promise, and honor, and integrity.

Lord, God, restore the legacy of love and promise in marriage and family, in mother and father, in children and grandparents. Heal the hurt and betrayal and confusion of broken family trust and help my children and grandchildren to wholly trust in You as their God and Savior. Forgive us for failing each other and our children by not being the best example of what it means to be in a marriage union, and as Christian parents. Lord, protect our children and grandchildren, and let them always know You as their Savior, their provider, their protector, and that You will love and care for them and never let them go. God, help us to trust in You as a child trusts in a good parent.

God, help us to rest in Your peace and to not be anxious about anything, for all things are possible with

You, God. And we know that all things work for the good of those who love the Lord, and we love You, Lord. Thank You that You have a good plan for me, my husband, my marriage, my family, and my future.

Lord, help me to live in this moment of the present, as a gift from You. Let me live each moment for You and to do my best for You as I love and help others without the motive of selfish gain. Father God, help me to not remember my past through the veil and lens of pain and bitterness, but, Lord, exchange my hurt, bitterness, and anger with Your grace, Your forgiveness, Your mercy, and Your loving joy.

Heavenly Father, help me to realize You made me on purpose, with a purpose, and You see me as Your good and beautiful creation. Because You created me, I am Your perfect and treasured masterpiece. Because of the price You paid on the cross, Jesus, You said I am valuable and worth being rescued and redeemed, and You exchanged Your spotless and sinless life as a ransom for mine. Thank You, Lord, for Your forgiving blood, and that when we repent of our sin, we can come back into alignment and relationship with You, with the God of the universe, as You intended in the Garden. Thank You that You regard us like a pearl and a treasure of great price. Jesus, thank You that You found me worthy of rescuing and saving.

Thank You, Lord, that I have an eternal home with You, and I am part of the family of God. I am a child of God and know we have a great inheritance far superior to any inheritance provided by our earthly family. Our family trust is in You. I trust that You are holding me and that I am never alone, for You are with me. Father, God, I put my faith and hope and trust in You, and not in man. You, God, are my provider, my deliverer, and the lover of my soul.

Thank You, heavenly Father, for Your unconditional love and forgiveness, and help me to extend that same love and forgiveness to those who have hurt me, abandoned me, and rejected me. God, You said You hate divorce, and it is Your will for Your children, husbands and wives to be reconciled, healed, and restored together in love, and I know that is Your will. Your will is that the church would be the example of the Bride of Christ, and You intended for the husband to love the wife as Christ loves the church. I pray that Your will be done.

Jesus, You are my Savior, my deliverer, my counsel, and my friend. Lord, Your Word is a lamp unto my feet, and Your sacrifice has delivered me from the grave. I thank You that You are a good God and good Father Who wants His best for His children. You call me Your own, Your child, and You call me Your beloved. Thank You, Abba Father.

Lord, I trust in You and thank You for calling me Your beloved one. I will not be ashamed because of Christ, and I will let my light shine. I will let You, God, fight my battles in the heavenlies, for You have the triumph and the victory over the grave and over my enemies. We know the ending of the story. You've already won the battle at the cross. Jesus, You paid the price for our redemption, and with Your final breath, Jesus, You declared and decreed, "It is finished. The battle is over."

The end, amen and amen, so be it so.

Chapter 45

THE AWAKENING: SEPTEMBER 5, 2023

Dear Younger Me,

Are you still sleeping? Hear me as your soul awakens you to this new day. There's a clear and bright light when the subconscious resurfaces and wakes up the conscious mind to reality. When you experience the undercurrents of suppressed pain and hurt, you can sometimes feel anger and bitterness, confusion, and anxiety, but you may not always understand why you are having those feelings and triggered emotions. You live for years in that dark closet of despair and the unexpressed and suppressed emotions caused by hurt, betrayal, and rejection within the unacknowledged parts of the soul.

I whisper in your ear the words and pictures as the Holy Spirit resides in your soul and communicates to awaken you in your subconscious dreams.

Dear Younger Me,

He speaks to you in your dreams. You said, "Lord, I have nothing left; you've taken it all away. I lost my joy, my song, my dance, and my energy to fuel the purpose of my being. I don't know where to turn, Lord, because I don't know which way to go. I am stopped, Lord. I fell, he pushed me, I hurt, my breath faded, and my heart stopped. I give up! I surrender.

"You've taken me to this quiet place where I am alone, but to listen, to listen to You, God, and to hear Your will for this new life You brought me into. Lord, my motor has stopped on my boat of life, and I want no more but to float in Your sailboat and upon Your ocean of truth and love. Lord, I just embrace floating and being quiet and at peace with You. I am still. I wait, in Your will and Your peace. Be the wind in my sails.

Holy Spirit, be the breath that I breathe and the lifeblood of Jesus's saving grace that pulsates my heart back to life. I wait on You, my Lord Jesus. I listen and I wait, and I breathe quietly to hear Your whisper."

Dear Younger Me,
It's in that quiet prayer to the Lord where you will find peaceful rest in the safety of God's protective hand that will never let you go. It's in your higher intuition and the whispers of the Holy Spirit that is born through studying the word of truth and using it as your plumb line to recognize deception and differentiate the lie from the truth.

You've been fed the lie and embraced the deception, until now. Wake up. Come back to life, dear Younger Me. You've seen the lies in your past and how they've crumbled the core foundation of that house you lived in. You've made home to that life of the juxtaposed labors of the iron fist and the crumbling foundations of clay and shifting sand. The outcome of that house you've lived in can only bring destruction and pain.

Dear Younger Me,

You will recognize this misaligned purpose you've lived in, that God has called you out of. You've experienced the aftermath of the destructive, sinful lies. The remnants of the ash from the sin are a reminder of the fire that burnt you, your marriage, your home, and your family. The destructive fires of betrayal made you cry, kick, and scream within, but with God, you will become new, and you will walk through those fires unsinged.

God created emotions, and you need to feel them and let the pain out in a healthy way. It's in the things that break your heart, make you cry, and stir up righteous anger from within, that you will discover God's will and be aligned with your identity, your destiny, and your purpose in Christ. It's when you recognize your identity in Christ and embrace the truth of our faulty humanity that your subconscious mind and your nighttime dreams will merge with your conscious mind and your daytime reality. Understanding the truth and your memories of the past will become a fact of acceptance rather than a continued painful feeling. Remove the façade and the persona, and dispel the lies you were willing to accept.

You never knew you'd crash at the unexpected intersection of Expectant Dreams Drive and Perplexity Junction. This was your life's journey not done to you, but for you. I know you were overwhelmed with pain and the helpless and hopeless feeling of defeat. You were abandoned and rejected by man, and Jesus knows; He was there too. Many have been through these same fires of painful paths and dashed dreams.

You are a fifty-seven-year-old mom of four grown daughters, and a young grandma of six beautiful grandchildren. Now that you've come through this great and painful divorce after being married for thirty-four years, don't let divorce define you. You are now past and on the other side of this mountain of grief. The trials you've gone through brought you into this new place of maturity and courageous confidence.

You realize that every wrong choice, every traumatic event, and every change in life needs to be processed, felt, and embraced, if you are to learn from the experiences and overcome the perception of self-doubt and defeat. There is a transformational change and healing process that takes place in the hand of God. He loves you unconditionally.

After we've come through the fires of false beliefs, destructive deception, and misunderstood mindsets, we can embrace a newness in the learning and healing process. You've become more aware of the fact that we're all complex human beings with conscious and unconscious souls that can act or react willingly or indirectly through our persona or selfish, egotistical pursuits. We can all be superficial or complex beings with emotional depth or confusing thoughts linked to our desires and dreams of the future and dark secrets of the past. You've discovered and realized your value in Christ, in nurture and nature. You've been forgiven, and you forgave. You can now embrace the light of discovery and evolve into a more empathic, and purposefully productive, individual in life, relation, family, and community.

This healing journey into wholeness has propelled you into understanding your dreams and your newfound purpose of wanting to help others on their own healing journey and into their own Well Day. You look forward to the rewarding process and development this path will lead you into. You will embark on new discoveries of your own. You will be awakened to the truths of the Bible and apply them with wisdom and discernment. Your fears and dreams, acknowledged, accepted, and understood, will become your living experience. We cannot change anything until we accept it as it is. Fly and be awake and live.

Dear Younger Me,

You've grown, and you've blossomed through your trials as you've resisted temptations that were intended to tear you down. Do not believe lies, and do not live in a false reality of idealism. Your seed of new beginning is opening from the fire that burned you. There's purpose in the fires we go through in life. There's rebirth and new beginnings that come through the fire and death of self. God is bringing you into this new day and a new love, a new plan, and a new purposeful beginning. You will see very soon. Just wait. Awaken and live. You will see.

Last night, you had a dream, dear Younger Me. You will dream it and remember it when your night merges into your new day of the here and now. When your subconscious crosses over to your conscious as the Holy Spirit whispers from within, you will be awake. When your night is over, your new day will dawn, and you will come back to life on purpose. Your mourning will turn into a new morning.

You will wake up to the dream where you were floating on a great and smooth body of water, just as a sailboat floats. Yet you had no boat; you had no motor, except for the Holy Spirit within. You were at peace and calm on the rippling water. You watched a raindrop as its upside-down image rippled out onto the water. You were afloat. Just you, flat out, supine, with your hands above your head, praising your Father above. You were afloat yet going nowhere in the calm waters. Until suddenly, a new energy and a breath of purposeful love and knowing fueled you and propelled you forward. You glided on top of the surface of the water, and you were enlivened by the forward motion. You knew you were heading in the direction purposed for you. You were finally on course with exhilarating speed.

You were at peace in this new forward motion, and you were courageous, bold, and unafraid of sinking insomuch that you stood up on top of the water and started to walk. You walked, you twirled, you sang, and you danced above the water.

You confirmed in your mind and heart, I will be true to my God, true to myself, and true to the ones I love, and I will be free to express my thoughts and give voice to my words. I will take a stand and fight for righteousness and freedoms for the oppressed, for the sake of families, and children, and our nation. I will give voice to reason wrapped in love. I will listen to the voice of God that propels me into purposeful action that makes a trajectory shift away from the malevolent ways of the world.

There's a calling that sounds an alarm to wake you up from your unconscious and unaware slumber. Wake up, oh, sleeping one. The hour is late. Arise, and let your light shine in the dark world and make a difference. Be the voice for the silenced, the abused, the manipulated, and the oppressed. Do not hit that snooze button. Wake up.

Dear Younger Me,
Breathe anew, and arise. You will shake off your slumber and weary ways of a traveler without direction. Open your eyes to the reality of this new day, and you will find love again. Take a stand, and be the music; be the song and the

voice that arouses and calls the oppressed from their hidden caves in the wayward wilderness. Arise. Wake up, dear Younger Me. For the legacy of truth, the voice of a child, and the freedom of faith, family, and nation. Wake up to this new day and the new reality of life as it is. Make a difference. Open your eyes. Breathe, fly, be alive. Be on purpose, dream, and live free once again. Be a living legacy, and become the new name you are given. You are Stephanie, and you are crowned with the garland of praise.

Then Stephanie Livingston breathed in and opened her eyes. She was now, once again, awake in her brave new world.

The end, and the new beginning.

Printed in the USA
CPSIA information can be obtained
at www.ICGtesting.com
JSHW021450091124
73282JS00001B/2